MASTERS

OF

MINECRAFT

The Awakening

by Terry Mayer

This novel is entirely a work of fiction.

The names, characters and incidents portrayed in it are the work of the author's imagination. Any resemblance to actual persons, living or dead, events or locations is entirely coincidental and all the characteristics of any player's mentioned are completely fabricated and are a figment of the authors imagination.

Masters of Minecraft is an unofficial Minecraft novel and is an original work of fan fiction that is not associated with Minecraft or MojangAB. It is an unofficial work and is not sanctioned nor has it been approved by the makers of Minecraft.

Minecraft is the official trademark of MojangAB.

Copyright © 2014 Terry Mayer

All rights reserved.

ISBN-13: 978-1495296482

ISBN-10: 1495296482

I dedicate this book to my wonderful daughter Sophie, without whom I would have been limited to Microsoft spellchecker.

Chapter 1

The Beginning

"Man, I love this game. Where else can you build an exact replica of a medieval castle, and even walk around it, he thinks walking up to the tower and climbing the battlements. All in survivor mode too, he exclaims, looking over the darkening countryside and seeing dozens of shambling zombies advancing on his defensive position. Hah, you can't get me you meatheads, he shouts.

Spotting a couple of creepers moving at the edge of the forest, he's a little more wary of them. Tall, green, stick like figures that run up to you and explode, they could be a bit more trouble if provoked. This is the most awesome build ever, exclaims Jay, with a huge smile on his face. It's only taken twenty-two days to build. Never has anyone built such a beauty on Minecraft so quickly. I truly am Jay Lightningbuilder.

"Jay, come here would you honey, I'm going out."

"Aurh mom, I'm in the middle of my game."

"Jay! I need to speak to you. Come here right now."

"But I've been playing for hours and it's not saved, can't it wait?"

"Jay. Come here now or you're banned from that game for the rest of your life, you hear me?"

"Yes mom," replies Jay sheepishly, saving his game and heaving himself off the couch, leaving a teenage sized imprint in the leather.

"Good, nice to finally see you back in the world of the living," says his mom as she fusses with his hair.

"Ah mom, give it a rest, it's the holidays. I don't need tidy hair to play Xbox. Nobody can see me, ok?"

"Well, there's no excuse for not looking your best Jay. Just because you're at home does not mean you have to be a slob now, does it?"

"No mom," he sighs.

"Good. Well I'm off to work and I have that meeting afterwards, so I will not be back until 11pm tonight, that means you're in charge, god help me," she says crossing herself. "Now Jack will be back in 5 minutes and he has his friend, Nathan, staying over, so I expect you to look after them today. Ok?"

"But mom, you know Jack's just a dweeb and he can't...."

"Jay Stephen Jacobs, you watch your mouth. That's my son you're talking about."

"I know mom, but he is a dweeb," whines Jay.

"Well, be that as it may, he is my son and he's your stepbrother, so I am putting you in charge, and you will look after him, or so help me god I will skin you alive, you hear me?"

"Yes mom."

"Good, now let him and Jack play on that Xbox thingy with you and you can all have some fun. There's pizza in the freezer and I put a six pack of coke in the fridge, so you guys be good, you hear?"

"Yeah okay, oh and mom?"

"Yes Jay?"

"Have a good day ok? I know it's a big meeting tonight, I really hope it goes well for you."

"Thank you Jay, it is important. If I'm lucky this could be the big promotion I've been waiting for."

"Cool mom, you'll do great, I just know it."

"Thanks Jay. Oh, here comes Jack and Nathan now. Be good, love you," and with that she pecks him on the head and dashes out the door.

"Well if it isn't dweeb 1 and dweeb 2. How's it going dweebs?" he smirks, as Jack and Nathan step into the house.

"Shut it Jay, we're not dweebs," responds Jack.

"Yeah, you want to make something of this, tough man?" shoots back Jay, stepping in front of his stepbrother.

"Mom said you had to be nice to us, so back off."

"No dweeb, mom said I had to look after you, she said nothing about being nice, so zip it before I close it permanently."

"You're not my boss; I don't have to listen to you."

"Is that right? Last chance dweeb, get in the living room and zip it or I'll show you who's the boss, right in front of your friend. How'd you like that?"

"I hate you!" screams Jack, running into the living room.

"Yeah, and what you looking at dweeb 2?" sneers Jay at Nathan.

"Uh nothing. I'm sorry sir. I was just going to join Jack in the living room, if that's ok with you."

"Sure, off you run now." I could get used to being called sir, he thinks, as he follows them in and takes his place on the couch.

"Right dweebs, this is Minecraft," he says as he turns his Xbox back on, "so watch and be amazed at a master in action."

"Master of nothing," sniggers Jack.

"I didn't quite hear that dweeb. You want to say that a little louder?"

"Uh no, it's ok."

"Good, so shut it unless you're spoken to. Now, as I was saying. This is Minecraft, one of the best games ever made. Also available on PC but personally I prefer the playability you get right here on the Xbox. Now dweeb 2, you familiar with this game?"

"No sir, I've never even heard of it."

"Stop calling him sir, he's just my brother Jay. It's creepy."

"What's up dweeb is it upsetting you that even your friend prefers me?"

"Cut it out Jay or I'll tell mom."

"Cut it out, cut it out. Man, you are such a dweeb. Anyway, as I was saying. Minecraft is a classic game and I am one of the very few people who can call themselves a master. Why, I hear you ask? Well let me tell you. I am a master of this game because I build bigger and better than anyone else does. In fact I am so awesome that I have received a personal invitation from The Notch to participate in a Masters of Minecraft Tournament this weekend."

"Yeah right Jay. Like The Notch even knows who you are."

"He sure does. In fact he's due to contact me anytime now."

"Seriously? The Notch is calling you. Way cool, just wait until I tell everyone tomorrow."

"Ah no, you can't do that, in fact I wasn't supposed to even tell you. It's some sort of secret."

"Excuse me sir, but who is this Notch person?"

"The Notch is just the greatest game designer who ever lived. He's the creator of Minecraft, not just some person, more like a GOD!"

"Oh! That sounds great."

"Great, great? Have you lost your mind? Great is when you get two bars from the vending machine by accident. Great is when you win a free drink at McDonalds but being invited to play in a Masters of Minecraft tournament by The Notch is super awesome beyond belief. Not great."

"Yes sir, now I understand, sorry."

Bending down Jay turns on the Xbox and turns to speak to his audience. "Right, now we've got that sorted let me show you my latest achievement. Not only is it super special but it was also built incredibly quickly. It took me just 22 days to build a design that would take a normal person many months." Reaching for the Xbox controller he continues, "now sit back and prepare to be dazzled."

"Oh Jay, you don't want to do that," stammers Jack.

"Shut it dweeb I'm really not talking to you again this evening."

"No seriously Jay, stop," shouts Jack.

"I'm not telling you again, shut it or I'm coming over there and shutting it for you," he snarls as he grasps the Xbox controller.

"No Jay, STOP!"

However, it's too late. Not looking at the controller Jay does not see that it has turned a bright, vivid green that seems to shimmer and fade in and out of focus. The moment his hand touches the pulsating object Jay spins around as a bright white pain shoots up his arm into his shoulders then into his forehead. Screaming in agony, he drops to his knees. "Jack, get it off me. It's eating me, quick Jack, help me please, help!"

Running to his side, Jack grabs Jays' arm, but the moment he touches him he is also struck with the same bright white pain that drives him to the floor. Screaming in agony the two brother's twitch on the floor, pulsating with a bright white light, this fades out to a green hue around the edges.

Seeing his friend in agony, Nathan jumps to his feet screaming. "Where's the electric box Jack, where's the power switch?" Receiving no answer from the lads, he runs to the kitchen and starts opening cabinets. On his third attempt, he finds the mains board behind a counter unit and flips the power off switch. Running back to the living room he is horrified to find the two lads still rolling on the floor, whitish green light pulsating around them.

"Nathan, what can I do? The power's off, you should be alright."

"Help me," moans Jack, reaching out his twitching hand. "Please help me."

"I don't know how!" screams Nathan. "What can I do?"

"Help me," he croaks again as his voice gets weaker. "Please help," and with a final twitch he throws his hand onto Nathan's leg.

Screaming, Nathan tries to jump back but he is too slow, and the moment Jack's hand makes contact with his leg there is a blinding flash of light and all goes dim.

*****

Chapter 2

The Awakening

Slowly coming to, Jay is amazed that he's not dead, although there is a strange whistling noise in his ears and he feels really weird. Almost like the time he jumped off the high board, down at the sports centre, except that this sensation just keeps on going. If it was really like jumping off the high board that would mean I've been falling for ages, from God knows how high, and if I'm falling that means I have to stop sometime, and that means a sudden stop with loads of blood and guts. No big deal usually but this time they would be my blood and guts.

"Arrhh," he screams. "Arrhh."

"Is that the best you've got?"

"What? Who said that, who's there?"

"Who said that, who's there? You dweeb."

"Jack, is that you?"

"Who else do you think it is?"

"I don't know. I woke up and it feels like I'm falling, and there's this rushing wind, and I was all alone and I didn't know what was happening, and, and, and...."

"Finished?"

"What's happening Jack?"

"We are falling, and we have been for at least an hour, could be more as we were already falling when I woke up."

"An hour, how can we be falling for an hour?"

"AN HOUR," mimics Jack, talking like Miss Totty in Curse of the Were Rabbit. "How can we be falling for AN HOUR?"

Laughing despite himself, Jay shouts. "But how can we be falling for so long?"

"No idea, I was hoping you would know what's going on."

"Why do you think I would know," he shouts back.

"Because whatever this is came from your game. When you pressed the button on the Xbox and the screen came on, this green glow seeped off the Minecraft logo on the screen and dripped onto the controller, so when you picked it up you were infected, or something."

"That's mad. You can't get infected from an Xbox game."

"I'm telling you Jay, that's what happened."

"Ok. So if I'm here because I'm infected by an Xbox game, how do you explain you being here?"

"Because when you started screaming like a little girl, I ran over to help you, but the moment I touched you I was infected too."

"That's rubbish. I never screamed like a girl."

"Get it off me Jack, it's eating me, Oh help," he giggles.

"Well, it hurt. What was I supposed to do?"

"No Jay, you're right. So what now?"

"What do you mean?"

"Come on Jay, we can't just stay here falling. I know it's pretty cool, but how are we going to get out of this mess?"

"Why are you asking me?"

"Because I'm twelve and you're my big brother. You're supposed to be looking after me. What do you think mom would say if she could see us now?"

At this, Jay bursts out laughing.

"What's so funny?"

"You, when you said 'what would mom say,' She would probably say something like I hope you put on clean underwear this morning, I don't want you boys having an accident with dirty underwear."

"Yeah or 'Don't go messing around in those clouds, you don't know where they have been."

"Yeah right. Oh, what clouds?"

"Just below us, those white things look like clouds."

"That's not clouds, they're glowing and pulsating."

"Oh no Jay, that's just like when you touched the controller and we're heading straight for it."

"What can we do?"

"Don't ask me, you're supposed to be in charge."

Momentarily forgetting where he is, Jay turns his head to Jack. "Oh, so now I'm in charge. When we're hurtling through space, at who knows how fast, with no way of stopping, then suddenly, I'm in charge. Perfect timing Jack, just perfect."

At just that moment, the brothers slam into the cloud formation, which splits on contact to reveal the earth rushing up to meet them.

"Arrrgggh," screams Jay, just before slamming into the green field, leaving a crater the size of a football pitch.

"No," screams Jack as he hits the white coastal rocks, at what must be a couple of hundred miles an hour, exploding rock shooting into the air.

Time passes in a blur for Jay. Images come and go at the edge of his vision, indistinct sounds surround him, and he has no idea if he is even alive. A vibrating sensation arouses him and he raises his head, and as his vision clears. He is amazed, not only is he still alive, but there are also enormous letters floating in the sky, which read.

You have been respawned - start again.

*****

Chapter 3

Respawned

Bewildered, Jay hardly notices the constant tapping on his shoulder. Finally realizing that it's Jack annoying him, he turns and shouts. "Give it a break Jack, I just died, can't you just give me five minutes..." He stops in mid sentence, staring at his brother; at least he thinks it's his brother. "What the heck?"

"I know Jay, you too. Take a look at yourself."

"What? What's happening here," he stammers looking down at where his hands should be, but they are now all square and blocky. "What's wrong with me Jack, and what's wrong with you?"

"We're blocks Jay. Just like in your game. We're in Minecraft."

"But that's impossible. It's just a game. This only happens in the movies."

"Too bad Jay because it's real. Look at yourself then look at me. I'm a block."

Looking up, Jay takes in what Jack is saying. He's not wrong; as they are both, for whatever reason, block men. Stocky, cube shaped people that inhabit the world of minecraft.

"But how Jack, and what's that crazy respawned stuff up in the sky?"

15

"Come on Jay. You've played this a million times; this is how it starts each time after you die."

"So we're dead?"

"I don't think so. In fact, this sounds weird, but I think we've just been reborn into this world. Respawned, if you like."

"Awesome." Looking around, Jay surveys his immediate surroundings. "Hey, this looks like right at the beginning, when you first start. If I'm right, the sea is just over those hills," he says, pointing out a low hill line in the distance.

"So, what do we do Jay?" asks Jack, feeling relieved that Jay was back to himself.

"Right, so if you're right, and we really are in Minecraft, then we have to play the game, at least until we can figure out what's happening?"

"Ok, so you're the master, what do we do first?"

"Right, first off we need to build a shelter. We've no idea what mode we are playing in, survival or creative, so we don't want to be wandering around when it gets dark."

"Why not?"

"Because this is a game, and in that game, monsters come out at night. Zombies that will eat you, skeletons that will kill you with a sword or arrow and don't get me started on creepers which just blow up everything around them."

"Uh, Jay, you really think there will be monsters here?"

"You can count on it, but we call them mobs, anything that can kill you is a mob."

"Ok, but what can we do?"

"First of all, just like I said, let's get a shelter built then at least we'll be safe tonight. You go get some wood, just hit the trees with your fists and it should come apart. I'm going to scout around quickly for a good place to build. Meet back here in five minutes, alright?"

"Ok, how much wood do we need?"

"As much as you can, quick as you can too. We don't know how much time we have."

"Right, see you in five."

Walking towards the hill line, Jay is amazed at the feel of the place. He has wandered through terrain such as this so many times before, but actually, being here and experiencing it first hand is just awesome. Hearing a thud to his right he heads over towards a small outcrop and peers around the side. Lying in a heap is another block man, just like himself.

"Hey, Steve, what's up man?" shouts Jay. Steve is the name of the avatar everyone inhabits in Minecraft.

"Oh sir, is that you? What's happening, where are we?"

"Dweeb 2, is that you. How come you're here?"

"I've no idea where here is, and the name is Nathan."

"Right, like I said, Dweeb 2. Looks like we are in this together now, so come on. I'll explain on the way."

Running over to Jay, Nathan asks. "On the way to where sir?"

Stopping and looking at him, Jay replies. "Right, first, quit calling me sir. It was cool at first but now it's real old. Second, it seems we have been pulled inside my Xbox and are now playing Minecraft for real."

"Really, but how?"

"No idea, but that's not important right now, but what is, is getting a shelter built. Right, let's get back to Jack and get started."

"Jack's here too?"

"Yep, all three of us got dragged in somehow. Let's go."

17

Walking back the way he came, Jay freezes as more enormous letters light up the sky.

You have been respawned - start again.

Oh no, Jack, he thinks running back to where he left his brother.

"Jack. Jack. Where are you Jack?" he shouts as he heads back into the clearing.

"Over here, what's up?"

"You're ok? I thought you were dead."

"I'm fine. Why'd you think I was dead?"

"Because it said you had been respawned."

"Nope, not me. You think someone else is here?"

As he asks this, Nathan comes jogging into the clearing.

"Nathan, is that you?"

"Yep, every little block of me," he replies laughing.

"Cool, great to see you man. There you go, it was Nathan who respawned."

"Yeah, yeah. Kisses all round. I had already found Nathan before the sky lit up, and if you're ok, then who was respawned?"

"Don't know, but if all three of us made it here, then maybe someone else is here too. Do you think we should try to find them?"

"No, we don't have time. We need to get a shelter built, right now. I hope that whoever came through knows how to play and will know what to do. Right, Jack, how much wood have you got?"

"Loads Jay, here's 16 chunks. Do you want me to get more?"

"Yeah, and take Nathan with you, show him what to do. I'm going to start on the shelter."

Picking up the wooden blocks that Jack dropped, Jay quickly breaks them down into planks. Then taking four planks, he makes a crafting table. Cool, this is just like playing, he thinks. Right, let's get some basic tools sorted. Picking up a plank, he breaks it down into poles then arranges two poles end to end on his crafting table, adds three wooden planks and hey presto, an axe. Way cool!

"Hey Jack, come here. I've got an axe to help you." Quickly building a pickaxe, he hands one each to Jack and Nathan as they jog back into camp and drop a load more wooden chunks on the floor.

"Cool Jay, how'd you make that, can you show me?"

"No time now, I'll show you tonight. Right, more wood Jack, and Nathan try to get some stone, quick as you can, and don't wander off too far."

Right, time for a shelter, 7 x 7 should work for tonight. Might be a tight squeeze but should be ok. Digging out a foundation with his new pickaxe, he starts laying cobblestone blocks to build a wall. Raising two blocks high he encloses himself and looks up. I better make a door so the others can get in he laughs. Laying out six boards on the crafting table a door magically appears, it's the only word that seems appropriate to Jay, even though he has been building on Minecraft for years, seeing it with his own eyes is something else.

Putting it in place, Jay starts on the roof just as Jack and Nathan return with more supplies.

"Jay, it's getting dark and there's something moving around out there," stammers Jack.

"What was it, could you see?"

"No, I just heard it moving around. You think it's the monsters already?"

"Probably, come on, get inside, and let's not take any chances."

"Monsters, what do you mean monsters?" chokes Nathan.

"Jay reckons that there are skeletons, zombies, and some creep out there trying to kill us."

"Not some creep, a creeper. It's a tall, green thing that chases you and when it gets close enough explodes and kills everything around it."

"For real? Monsters?"

"Yep, sorry Nathan. That's why we had to get this shelter built real quickly."

"Will we be safe here?"

"Yeah, we just have to stay inside until sun-up and we'll be ok. Right, let's get this roof finished before it rains then I'll make a furnace so we can have a bit of heat, and then I can make some charcoal so we can make torches."

Working furiously, Jay completes his tasks then settles down for the evening.

"So Jay, what's happening, why are we here?" asks Jack.

"I'm not 100 percent sure, but I have been thinking about it this afternoon. It must have been that invitation I received from The Notch, but how we have actually ended up here, I've no idea."

"So you think we are in a tournament?"

"Maybe, I can't think of anything else."

"Ok, if that's right, then what do we have to do? What are the rules and how do we win?"

"Good questions little brother and I don't have the answers. I usually play in creative mode where there are no mobs, so I don't know what we are supposed to accomplish here."

"How can we play if we don't know the rules? This is mad, even being here is mad."

"I know Nathan, but I'm sure we will work it out tomorrow."

"Tomorrow! Jay, mum is coming home tonight. If we are not home when she gets there she's going to freak and call the police. We need to get home tonight," shouts Jack jumping up from the floor.

"Chill Jack, Minecraft time is different from human time. Here a day is only two hours in human time so we can spend a few days here before anyone will even miss us back home."

"A few days Jay, I don't know whether to be happy or upset at that thought."

"Yeah I know what you mean, but let's just get some rest because something tells me we are going to need all our energy tomorrow."

*****

Chapter 4

Welcome To The Tournament

Waking with a start, Jay looks around groggily. Where am I, what's going on. Bleary eyed he surveys his surroundings. Four walls, a roof, a small furnace in the corner, a couple of Steve's asleep on the floor. What! Jumping up he notices his hands and recognition floods his overloaded brain. Oh no. I'm really here and it's not a dream.

BOOM.

There it is again, that must have been what woke me.

BOOM.

What is it? Opening the door just a crack, not sure if it was still night, Jay peers outside. Relieved that darkness has given way to daylight, he pulls open the door and steps outside.

BOOM.

There it is again.

"What's that noise Jay?"

Turning he sees Jack has come out of the house, and is standing behind him.

"Don't know Jack, I've never heard it before."

BOOM... BOOM.

"It's getting faster Jay, you think that means something?"

BOOM, BOOM, BOOM.

BOOM, BOOM, BOOM.

BOOM, BOOM, BOOM.

"I don't know. I can hardly hear myself think," he shouts over the crashing, vibrating, and thunderous explosions of noise. It's like ..."

Silence, the explosions stop while Jay is in mid sentence.

"What now?" he asks looking around. Just then a huge thunderous voice cracks the silence.

Welcome to the 'Masters of Minecraft' Tournament.

Each one of you has been personally invited to participate in this hardcore event. It is a great honor, reserved for the greatest twelve players the earth has to offer, to battle it out to find the ultimate, Master of Minecraft.

The rules are few.

You need to build and stay alive.

A canon will precede any important announcements, such as a player death, or a new challenge.

Good luck and let the tournament begin.

BOOM.

"That's it, build and stay alive. What are we supposed to do?" shrieks

Nathan.

"Just like the guy said, build, and stay alive. That's Minecraft. No real rules, no objectives, just get on with it."

"Yeah, but he said that the twelve best players were here. I've never even played before and Jack's not exactly world class, so what are we doing here?"

"Don't know, but it must have been when you both grabbed hold of me, you must have been sucked through by mistake."

"Great, so who do we complain to then Jay," asks Jack, joining in the conversation.

"Don't know, Jack the dweeb," sniggers Jay.

"Cut it out Jay, now is not the time to be taking the ..."

"No Jack, look up. That's your name."

Looking up, Jack sees his name hovering over his head. Jack the Dweeb. "Oh that's just great. Even the game's mocking me."

"Yeah, look at Nathan the Noob. Guess you guys are playing too."

"Great, so we get stuck with dweeb and noob and you get Jay Lightningbuilder. Not fair."

"No, I think that sounds about right. As I told you before. The reason that I was invited is because I am the quickest builder in minecraft. I reckon we have about an hour until dark, let us get building. Jack, go fetch wood, Jay, get more cobblestone. Move quickly, keep your wits about you, and for Notch's sake don't let anyone see you."

"Why not, we're all here together, why can't we talk to the others, see if they know what's going on?"

"Because Noob, this is a tournament and they might just kill you, ok?"

"For real?"

"Yeah, for real, and this is hardcore which means permadeath, no respawning."

"So what happens if we die?" asks Jack, jumping into the conversation.

"Don't know, hopefully we just go home, but ..."

"So why don't we just get ourselves killed and get out of here?" he butts in once again.

"Because, if you had let me finish, I said I don't know what happens. This is all unheard-of, who's to say what happens, and maybe we really die!"

"Oh no, you think?"

"Don't know, but let's not take any chances. Now go, daylight's burning here. Keep your eyes open for any lava fields; we need to start mining as soon as possible."

Both Jack and Nathan run in different directions to start collecting materials, while Jay takes in his surroundings. What the heck have we gotten ourselves into now? Right, the first job is to fortify this building. Working at a flat out pace, Jay builds another structure alongside the first and connects the two together, and then he builds a balcony on the roof to allow him to view outside at night without having to open the door. Right, weapons. Moving to his crafting table Jay makes three short swords, using two cobblestones and a pole. I guess these will have to do for now. Stone swords are not the best of weapons, but we have nothing else. Just as he finishes, Jack returns with a haul of wood.

"Wow Jay, that's amazing! I've only been gone a few minutes and you've built another house. Cool."

"Cheers Jack, how's it going out there?"

"Good, but I broke my axe," he says a little downbeat.

"No probs bro, I'll make another, they don't last long anyway." Handing Jack his new axe he also gives him a sword. "Here, it's for defense only, remember what I said about staying hidden?"

"Yeah, I saw no one anyway."

"Good, off you go now and look out for any animals; we are going to have to eat soon."

"What do I do if I see one Jay?"

"If it's a pig or a cow then kill it."

"Yuk, gross Jay."

"Nah, it's really simple. Once you kill it, it will turn to pork or beef; just bring it back here, ok?"

"Right, I'm off again."

Running from the house Jack heads back to the woods in search of more wood, and hopefully something for dinner."

Jay continues to build while waiting for Nathan to return. Constructing a hoe, he moves outside and clears some ground ready for planting, then moving into a grassy area he collects some grass, snaps it in half, and harvests the seeds. Planting them in the cleared area he stops and smiles. Cool, now we should have some food. Just then, Nathan runs back into camp.

"Jay, Jay, look what I found."

"Hey Nate, what's up man?"

Throwing his stash on the floor, he grabs Jay's arm and shows him his haul. "Look, loads of stone and I think that's coal, is it Jay?"

"Yes Nate, that's coal. Well done, is there more where you found that?"

"Yeah there are loads, and look, I got loads of string."

"Where did you find that?" asks Jay a little worried.

"Down where I found the coal, in this little cave. It looked like cobwebs but when I pulled it, it came away like this, cool huh?"

"Yeah Nate, but where there's cobwebs, there's spiders, and in Minecraft, spiders can kill you."

"I never thought of that."

"No probs. Spiders make this clicking sound when they are near, so if you hear anything just grab your stuff and get back here ok?"

"Right Jay."

"Good. Here's a sword to defend yourself with, just try not to use it unless you have to. Now when you're out, if you see any animals get back here and show me real quick. Now off you go as we only have about half an hour of daylight left."

"Ok Jay," shouts Nathan over his shoulder, as he runs off again.

"I think he's actually enjoying himself," he smirks to himself.

Over the course of the next half hour, Jay continues to construct a fence around his garden and a fenced area ready for animals if they are lucky enough to catch some. Jack returns with more wood and a pile of pork from his first kill. Then Nathan returns with more stone, some more string, and a chicken.

"Cool Nate, where did you find the chicken?"

"It was just wandering around so I walked over and picked it up, real easy," he beamed. "Is it any use?"

"Sure is. We can get eggs from it, meat when we need it and feathers. Way to go guys looks like we might just survive another night, and speaking of night the sun is going down, so let's get inside."

Piling into the house, the lads all admire Jay's handiwork. Man, you really are Jay Lightningbuilder, aren't you?"

"Sure am bro, right, let's get some food. How are your health point's guys?"

"What do you mean?" they both ask looking at one another.

"Your health points. Take a look and see what you're on."

"How?" they both chime.

"You sort of look inside yourself. It's a bit weird at first, but you'll soon get the hang of it."

Concentrating hard, the two lads look like they are in pain, when suddenly Jack shouts.

"Hey, I can see, I'm almost full, just one missing."

"Well done Jack, me too, so all is good there. How about you Nathan?"

With a pained expression Nathan replies, "I can't see anything, what am I doing wrong?"

"You look like your in pain with your face all scrunched up like that," laughs Jay.

"Yeah Nate," laughs Jack.

"Quit it guys, I'm trying here," he moans.

"Just relax Nate, it's easy, just look inside yourself and you will see loads of information about yourself," sooths Jack, suddenly feeling sorry for his friend.

"Right, I got it, cool," squeaks Nate. "I've got two life points left, why so few?"

"Only two, what happened to you?"

"Nothing Jay, I was just collecting cobblestone and the like, jumping around in the cave, nothing happened."

"When you say jumping, did you fall or anything?"

"Yeah, but I never got hurt, it just sort of made me shake, so I carried on."

"Nate, that shaking is your health points disappearing. Two more falls and you would be dead."

"What? But I never hurt myself."

"You did Nate, it's just here you don't feel bad or go to the doctor, you just die! Right, let's get some food cooked quickly and rebuild your points." Saying this, Jay gets up and starts a fire in the furnace using some of Nathan's coal, and cooks the pork. "Get this down your throat mate," he says handing Nathan a steaming pile of pork. After Nathan consumes every piece, he asks. "How are your life points now?"

Looking into himself, Nathan smiles, and shouts. "Cool Jay, all the way back up. That's awesome."

"Sure is, right Jack, you eat this one and put the other two in your packs guys," he says handing the lads some more pork. "We need to keep food on us at all times, just in case we get hurt, ok?"

"Yes Jay," they both answer.

"Good, now come over here and I'll teach you both how to use a crafting table," he says eating his own pork as he crosses the room.

For the next half hour, the lads huddle over the crafting table as Jay demonstrates how to combine different resources to make some basic tools. He demonstrates that by combining three poles and a string he can make a bow, eight blocks of wood to make a chest and seven poles to make a ladder.

"Right lads, you get the basic idea how this works, now so let's get some sleep ready for tomorrow."

"Ok Jay and thanks," says Nathan.

"What for Nate?"

"For looking out for us, I mean me. I think I would already be dead if I were on my own."

"No probs Nate. Now get some sleep," he smiles; secretly chuffed that

Nate appreciated him.

*****

Chapter 5

First Blood

Moving stealthily, Darknight creeps along the edge of the rocky outcrop. He has his sights on the large cabin just by the woods. Not one to be content building, Darknight prefers direct action and plans on eliminating his opponents in the old fashion way, chop them to bits and move on to the next. While the other competitors have been concentrating on building structures and making defensible positions he has spent his time mining and building. He has already crafted an iron sword and a bow and some leather armor and plans to take down his first opponent, steal their dwelling and make some better weapons.

With full health, Darknight is poised for action as he bends and scurries past the cave opening. Sensing something in the shadows, he turns, but is too late as an arrow slams into his shoulder, the impact rolling him past the opening. Rotten skeletons, he thinks, wondering whether to kill it or leave it for later. Stuff it, it's still daylight and I've enough to do, he decides as he pulls the arrow out with a grunt. These things hurt, he says, hurling it into the bushes.

Carrying on towards the structure he observers a fat avatar banging in fence posts outside his cabin, happily unaware that he has bad company lurking just out of his line of sight. Oh good, it's Jethro Skybuilder he mouths, looking at the floating name above his head. He may be one hell of a constructor but he sure has no clue about defense. Creeping along the tree line, he closes his position from the rear to prevent Jethro Skybuilder from escaping back into his cabin. Placing three arrows in the ground for quick access he notches his last arrow, loosens his sword in his scabbard and breaths deep, readying himself for the offensive. This should be quick and painless; at least for me he chuckles.

Breathing out he takes aim on Jethro Skybuilder's back and let's fly the first arrow, immediately notching the second and letting loose also. Reaching for the third arrow, excruciating pain explodes in his back. He falls to the grounds as another explosion of pain rips through him. Screaming in agony, he jumps to his feet, expecting to see another assailant bearing down on him but there is no one in sight. Quickly assessing the situation, no other assailant, the skeleton must have got a bead on me somehow, he rushes forward to finish off Jethro before he can escape.

Looking up from the ground in agony, Jethro sees, to his horror, an armored avatar rushing at him, sword lifted above his head readying a killing blow. Screaming, he tries to defend himself, diverting the killing blow, but knocking his health down to just two points.

As Darknight slashes at his prone victim, Jethro raises his arm in defense and diverts the blow. Grimacing as another white light of pain rips through him, this time in his arm, he stumbles but regains his balance ready to strike one final time.

"You are one hard avatar to kill Jethro Skybuilder, but your time in this game is over," he says standing above him, raising his sword in two hands, readying himself to strike straight down with a killing blow. "Prepare to meet your maker, fat boy," he chuckles as he thrusts downwards into Jethro Skybuilder's chest.

Screaming as the sword pierces his chest, Jethro Skybuilder looks into Darknight's eyes and sees doom, but strangely, not his own. His health is hanging precariously on one point but Darknight lets out an almighty scream and vanishes in a flash of brilliant light.

BOOM. The canon sound explodes in the air and then the

thunderous voice announces...

The first competitor has been eliminated. Darknight has not proven worthy. Eleven competitors remain. Continue the tournament.

Watching from the woods, Nathan cannot believe what he has just witnessed. Jethro Skybuilder should be dead. Darknight had him dead to rights, first with the arrows then the sword attack but Jethro survived and Darknight died. Not really thinking he jumps from his hiding place and dashes over to Jethro, reaching down to help him as he struggles to his feet.

Sensing another presence, Jethro turns in stunned horror as another avatar reaches out to him. "No, get back, leave me alone. Why can't you leave me alone?" he wails.

"Relax, it's ok, I'm here to help" sooths Nathan." I can't believe you're still alive. Here let me help you up," he says reaching out his hand.

Slapping the hand away, Jethro screams into his face. "Get away from me, don't touch me you just trolling."

"No really, I just want to help. Here, give me your hand and I'll help you back to your cabin."

Nearly passing out, Jethro stumbles into Nathan's outstretched arms. "You really aren't going to kill me?" he mumbles.

"Not today," he chuckles "but can't promise about tomorrow."

"What?" shrieks Jethro, trying to pull himself free?

"Calm down, I'm just joking. Now come on, let's get you inside before someone else takes a swing at you." Half dragging him, Nathan manages to get Jethro inside the cabin and drop him on his bed. "Cool cabin Jethro, real homely, you have been a busy boy."

"Yeah, yeah, just pass me some meat and bread quick, my health is almost gone." Grabbing the offered food, he wolfs it down in seconds and almost immediately, color returns to his face. "Ah yes, that's better, what the heck just happened?"

"I was going to ask you the same thing. I was watching from the woods when Darknight crept up on you, but before I could shout a warning he fired two arrows into your back, but then the strangest thing happened. It was just as if he shot himself. He was thrown forward and screamed in pain at the precise same moment that you did. Then he rushed forward and slashed at you with his sword and as he struck you, he screamed the same as you. Then you know the rest, the blow killed him and he vanished."

"Interesting, it seems that competitors that attack another competitor inflict the same damage on themselves, but why did he die and I live. I was on full health and I assume he was too?"

"No, that's it," shouts Nathan jumping up from his squatting position. "Just before he attacked you he was shot in the shoulder when he crept past that cave behind your house. He was already hurt when he started the attack, so if you both lost equal health points then his ran out first."

"Well, well, you may be right, pure luck on my part but I sure am glad to be alive. I never thought a game could be so painful." Jumping to his feet, rejuvenated after his food he holds out his hand. "Jethro Skybuilder at your service. I see you are Nathan the Noob. Not a great name for a Masters of Minecraft competitor."

"No, it sucks, in fact I shouldn't even be here," he moans, going on to explain how he had never even heard of Minecraft before yesterday, then getting dragged here with Jay.

"Well you are in a pickle, aren't you? However, you are with Jay Lighningbuilder, a good player and a nice fellow to boot. Well, well, what to do now, hmm."

"No idea, but I better get back before they start wondering where I am."

"Yes, yes, you run along now and really, I'm in your debt. If you ever need any help you can rely on me, not like that trolling avatar Darknight."

"Thanks Jethro, you take care of yourself and maybe I'll see you around," he shouts over his shoulder as he dashes off into the woods in search of his friends.

"My, my, what an enchanting fellow," smiles Jethro as he grabs some more food. "I sure hope he survives, but alas, I suspect that will be the last I see of him."

*****

Chapter 6

Stockholm, Sweden

Knocking on the office door Steve pokes his head around the door jam and addresses the man at the desk. "Hey Notch, you got a minute?"

"Sure Steve, come on in. What's up?"

"Well, there's something strange going on with the Minecraft servers, it's almost..."

Interrupting him in mid sentence Notch interjects. "Come on Steve, you know I've stepped away from Minecraft to concentrate on other projects, that's why I put you in charge."

"Yeah I know Notch, and normally I would not have bothered you but this is extreme in the most extremely weird way."

"Oh! I'm interested, so what's going on?"

"Right, a little earlier a game started on the server that we could not identify, but it's been sucking all the servers in and closing out other games as it grows."

"Really? That's a little weird, a hacker maybe?"

"If it is, he's good because we just can't locate him."

"Right, so how many servers are affected?"

"All of them!"

"What! How can they all be affected? There are so many fail safes built in that it's impossible."

"Yeah, well tell that to the servers, because right now they are all being used to play Masters of Minecraft."

"What did you say?"

"That all of the servers..."

"No, no, what game is it running?"

"Masters of Minecraft, why, you know something about this?"

"Sort of, I got an email this morning inviting me to play in this game but I figured it was a hacker. I was going to bring it up later this afternoon."

"Why, what made you think you were hacked?"

"Because it came from me, on my private email account."

"Ah Notch, you should have told me this morning."

"Yeah I know but I figured it was just a hacker messing with me, no harm done."

"Yeah, well there's a whole heap of harm coming down now, what do you want to do?"

"Reboot the servers and use our scan, wipe it clean and use the back-up if you need to."

"Tried that already, but we're locked out. All I get is, and I quote; 'Only invited players can participate at this time. Minecraft will resume at the completion of the tournament. Sorry for any inconvenience.'"

"You're kidding me?"

"Do I look like I'm joking?"

"Show me," he replies grabbing his laptop and bolting from the office, dashing down the hall to the server farm housed in the basement.

*****

Chapter 7
Tidal Wave

Running back into camp, Nathan stumbles into Jay and Jack staring out to sea. "Hey guys, you'll never guess what just happened."

"Darknight bought it, yeah I heard," mumbles Jay. "So you really think it is rising?"

"Yeah Jay, I know you say it can't happen but I swear the sea level has risen at least six blocks in the last five minutes."

"Guys I saw Darknight trying to kill Jethro and then he..."

"Hold up Nathan, this is important," interrupts Jay. "I think you're right Jack, the sea is coming in really fast."

"What do you think it means?"

"Normally I'd say that someone had added a mod pack and were messing with us but in this game we can't take any chances."

"So what should we do?"

Looking around at the lay of the land, Jay is concerned that there are no obvious high points on the horizon. "Well I guess we build a boat, and quickly, that sea is already half way to us. You two, give me any wood you have and go gather some more, quick as possible. Don't go too far, just get whatever you can as quick as you can, now go," he shouts dashing into the house and grabbing the crafting table.

Immediately turning the wood chunks on the floor into planks, he starts laying out the hull of a ship. Too small, too small, I can build anything I want here, not just the standard equipment, he mumbles tearing the craft apart and starting again, using a plan he had designed years earlier. I just hope I have enough time to make this.

As Jack returns to the cabin with the wood chunks he has collected he tells him to turn them into planks and pass them to him, then he continues knocking the hull together. Glancing over his shoulder, he sees the sea rushing towards him at an alarming pace. Nathan returns and makes Jay some more planks and hands them over, then dashes into the cabin to retrieve the furnace and the food supplies.

"Come on guys, not much more than a couple of minutes. Jack, quickly harvest the wheat, and put it on the boat. Nathan, grab everything left in the house and get it on board."

Working quicker than he had ever worked before, Jay finishes a makeshift hull and starts on making long poles so he can row and steer. No time for a sail, we will just have to make do with what we have. Hearing a thunderous rushing noise Jay glances towards the coast to see a wall of water rushing over the plains towards him.

"Get in the boat, now! Leave everything, come on come on," he screams as the lads jump on board.

Just as Nathan climbs in, the wall of water hits the prow of the boat at lifts it into the air, propelling it forward at a great speed of knots.

"Hold on, this is going to bumpy," Jay shouts out above the thunderous torrent. "Jack, grab that pole and get to the left, Nathan go on the other side and try and keep us from ramming into anything." Grabbing his own pole, Jay dashes to the stern of the craft and thrusts it between two vertical planks, anchoring the pole in place, so giving him a make shift rudder with which to steer.

"Watch out for those trees Nate, push us to the left," he screams over the thunderous noise. "Jack, watch out for obstacles, at the speed we're moving, we'll break apart if we hit something solid."

Thrusting the pole from side to side, Jay desperately tries to control the craft as it surfs along on the crest of the giant wave. "Right guys, on my count row backwards with everything you've got; if we go over the front edge of this thing we're doomed. Right, get ready, ROW!" he shouts at the top of his lungs.

At first there is no noticeable difference as all three lads continue to row, thrashing the water to a white torrent but ever so gradually the craft pulls away from the leading edge of the wave and starts to drop back from the precipice.

"Keep rowing, come on its working," screams Jay, trying to make himself heard, "almost there, keep going lads."

Gradually the craft slows, and the wave powers ahead of the craft leaving them in a storm of white water, but at least their progress starts to slow as the wave disappears over the hill line.

"That was too close," exclaims Nate. "Good call Jay, another thirty seconds, we would have been toast!"

"Yeah Jay, way to go bro!"

"Thanks guys but keep your eyes open; something tells me we haven't seen the last of that thing yet."

"But its gone Jay, what else is it going to do?"

"Don't know Nate, but nothing works like it's supposed to so expect the unexpected."

*****

Digging into the cobblestone with his iron pickaxe, Captain Sparkles continues to enlarge the chamber running off the deep tunnel he has excavated since the tournament began. There has to be some Redstone around here somewhere, a little diamond would not hurt either, he chuckles. Hearing a noise from behind he turns quickly. The chamber is still empty, no zombies creeping up on him, but the noise is still there, a moaning noise getting louder and louder. Running towards the tunnel, he is assaulted by a thunderous rushing noise, building in intensity with every step he takes towards the tunnel entrance. Reaching the opening, he peers tentatively around the corner just in time to see a wall of water rushing towards him from the top of the staircase. Jumping back, he immediately places cobblestone blocks across the mouth of the cave. As the water reaches him, he has only reached two blocks high and with a thunderous roar the wave of water smacks into the wall and rushes over the top. Working furiously he continues placing blocks, trying desperately to block the opening, while battling the ever increasing flow of water. Filing the last block at the top of the wall, he smiles to himself as the water ceases to flow. Is that all you've got? Blocking a flooding chamber is child's play, Masters of Minecraft tournament, NOT! he shouts at the ceiling. Strutting back into the cavern he does not notice the water starting to seep around the edges of the cobblestone blocks in the tunnel mouth.

*****

Placing the last cobblestone block on the tower wall, Natasha surveys her surroundings. One heck of a castle you have built yourself girl, she thinks. Staring out across the plains, something glistening on the horizon catches her eye. Ok, so what do we have here then? Looking closer she can see that it is moving, in fact not only is it moving, it's covering the whole of the horizon. Whatever it is, it is huge and getting closer. Mesmerized, she watches for a few seconds until suddenly her brain kicks into gear and she realizes what it is. Jumping from the tower and running to the front of the castle, she slams the doors just as the wall of water hits. Oh my God, that was close, I've never seen water like that in Minecraft. Just as she is thinking this, the doors start to bulge and water seeps around the edges. No way, this cannot happen. Placing a line of cobblestone in front of the door and sealing the entrance she runs back to the tower and climbs to the top. Looking out at the landscape, she gasps. Water covers the land as far as the eye can see.

*****

Looking up, Jethro Skybuilder wonders what the thunderous noise could be. Running from the newly constructed animal enclosure, he rounds the side of the house to see a rushing wall of water less than 20 blocks away. Turning he runs flat out towards his fortified home but the wave overtakes him in less than ten blocks. Picked up in the swirling mass of water, Jethro is tumbled and turned as he is swept along with the giant wave. Slamming into the side of the building he feels a health point flash and disappear. Oh dear, I could be in serious trouble here. If I can just get inside, I can survive this. Inch by inch he pulls himself along the front of the building as the power of the water tries to crush him flat. Making it to the door just as the water level reaches the top he ducks under, opens it, and the power of the water sweeps him into the building. Gasping for air as the water reaches the ceiling he heads for the stairs to the second level.

*****

Chapter 8

Stockholm, Sweden

"Right Steve, show me what the heck is going on" demands Notch.

"Ok, look here at the source code, according to this all the servers are now hardcoded into this game."

"But how, who wrote this code?"

"No one. Only the two of us have access to the source code for the main server and I'm guessing you didn't change it so that means we've been hacked."

"But it doesn't make sense. If we were hacked, we would not be able to gain access. All outside access has been suspended so either whoever hacked us has a back door or he has been locked out also. This is weird even for hackers."

"Yeah Notch, but that's not the worst of it, take a look at this," says Steve pulling the server from the rack.

"What the heck? The cables aren't even connected?"

"I know, told you it was weird. All the servers are communicating with Bluetooth, wireless, or something, who knows what, but there's no hardware installed. It's just not possible but it's happening."

"Right, shut it down. Everything, just turn it off."

"You sure Notch. We've never had to do that before."

"You ever had servers take over the game before?" asks Notch sarcastically.

"No. Ok, so how do we do this, there's no procedure in place for a shut down like this."

"Normally I would advocate backing up, and a gradual powered shut down, but I think we are way past the normal, so just press the power button and we'll worry about bringing it back on line when we have the hacks sorted out."

"Ok, here goes nothing," jokes Steve as he reaches forward to press the main power button on the front of the server. "What the heck, nothing's happening Notch."

"Yeah, guessed as much. Whoever hacked this now owns the servers, only option is to cut the power. Go on, pull the plug."

Pulling the server from its cradle, Steve reaches around the back and pulls the power lead out. Blinking rapidly he stares at the server, realizing that nothing is happening. "You have got to be kidding. It's still running, how's that even possible?"

"Pull it from the rack; make sure there are no other cables attached."

Pulling the server free and laying it on the floor Steve exclaims. "That's it Notch, she's completely isolated but still running. That is way beyond weird."

Staring at the server Notch looks perplexed. How can it still be running? The only possible explanation is we have been infiltrated. Someone must have installed a battery device into the server. "Right, open her up; there must be an independent power supply inside."

"But that's not possible; no one has access to these servers."

"But this is possible?" he retorts, pointing at the server laying on its side on the floor, all cables disconnected."

"No, I guess not." Grabbing a screwdriver, he starts removing the screws, securing the cover. "Ah Notch, this is getting weird," he stammers.

"What do you mean? This has been weird right from the start."

"Yeah, but get a look at this," he says removing the cover.

Looking into the server housing Notch gasps and takes a quick step back. "What the...?" Covering every square inch inside the case is a green, pulsating slime. "You have got to be kidding me! What the heck is that?" he splutters.

*****

Chapter 9

Watery Grave

Dragging himself up the stairs, Jethro takes a gasp of air just as his last health point is about to blink away. That was too close. Coughing up water, he stumbles over to his chest and retrieves some bread and pork. Eating ravenously, he feels his health returning. Glancing through the window, he sees a scene of utter devastation with water covering everything as far as the eye can see. Feeling a bump on the back of his legs he spins around, expecting the worst only to find that his chest has floated into him and he is standing almost waste deep in water. Glancing out the window again, he sees that the water has risen half way up the windowpane and is still rising. Picking up his chest, crafting table and furnace he heads for the roof. Man, it is so clever how much I can carry, its real life but with all the Minecraft bonuses. Standing on the roof of the building with the water still rising, Jethro realizes that his house will soon be under water. With nowhere left to go, he takes out his crafting table and makes a boat. Not a large, strong hull like Jay created but a standard Minecraft vessel. Climbing in, just as the water swallows the roof, he surveys his surroundings. So, what now, he wonders staring out onto endless water.

*****

Yes, Redstone. Digging out the blocks, Captain Sparkle's smiles to himself. Now I can really start constructing some worthwhile contraptions. Stepping off the block he was balanced on he is shocked to step back into waist deep water. Turning towards the tunnel entrance water is pouring around the edges of his makeshift wall, filling the room as he watches. That is not possible he thinks as he starts wading across the room to shore up the opening. After a few steps, he realizes that the room will be full of water before he gets to the tunnel entrance so turns and returns to his Redstone wall. Jumping up onto the ledge where he had been mining he starts digging upwards for 4 blocks then jumps in the air and places a block underneath himself. Moving at a steady pace, he continues building up 20 blocks before moving sideward and excavating a new chamber out of the cobblestone. Well, there goes my mine system, just have to start another one. Checking his inventory, he gasps as he realizes he has left his crafting table behind and has no wood to build a new one. Looks like it is a trip back to the surface to resupply, he thinks as he starts his upward journey once again.

*****

Watching the water creep up the walls of the castle, Natasha is shocked to see it start pouring over the battlements. Rushing to the edge of her tower, she looks around the outside walls only to see water pouring in from all directions. Realizing its pointless trying to save the whole castle, she decides to stick with just the tower. Jumping down to the castle wall, she starts to dig through the inner layer of cobblestone, storing each piece in her inventory. I am going to need every bit of cobblestone I can get if I am going to save this place, she thinks, digging like crazy. As the water reaches her knees, she climbs the steps to the tower and slams the door. Opening the door again, she pulls it from its hinges, tosses it inside, and then places six cobblestone blocks where it once sat. There, completely sealed, let us see what happens now; she grimaces as she starts the climb to the top of the 80 block tall tower.

*****

Man I went deep, thinks Captain Sparkles as he digs his way through another 20-block section. Keeping a uniform count, he had been digging upwards for twenty blocks, building a narrow one-block stair case then making a small 5 x 5 room and placing torches before starting up again. This way he would be able to check his progress when coming back down and giving him somewhere to stop and defend if he ran into any unpleasant situations. As he raises his pickaxe once again he pauses in mid swing, man almost made a noob mistake, he thinks as he stares at a wall of gravel. If

48

there's a flooded chamber above me and I take out a gravel block I could flood myself before I get a chance to repair the hole. Moving two blocks over on the cobblestone wall, he continues his long dig upwards.

*****

Removing the roof from the tower, Natasha is stunned at the speed that the water level has risen. Already 80 blocks high and the water's almost at the top, unbelievable. Storing the roof in her inventory, she starts to place more cobblestone blocks, raising the tower in a 2 x 2 winding staircase. Although slower to build than jumping up and placing a block underneath her, it gives the advantage of having a usable structure if she needs to go back down at any point. Building methodically, she raises herself another eighty blocks then stops and builds a small 5 x 5 platform before assessing her progress. She looks down in shock to see the water only five blocks below her. Picking up her pace, she continues to build higher and higher, although there is no sensation of height as the water follows her relentlessly. After building another 80-block section, she glances down and to her relief, sees that she is now ahead of the tide by 20 blocks. Either it is slowing down or I am getting faster, she thinks, sitting on the staircase watching the water below. After twenty minutes, the water is still at the same level and Natasha takes a great sigh of relief. Checking her inventory, she finds she still has over four hundred cobblestone blocks. Thank Notch that I collected so much cobblestone before the water hit or I would never have survived. After checking that the water level had not moved again, she builds a 7 x 7 platform at the top of the staircase. Building a two block high wall all around the structure she then reaches into her inventory and puts the roof on the building. Then starting a new staircase she builds another 20 blocks high, and places torches all around the outside, just in case she needs to get out quickly in the fast approaching night. Sitting on top of the staircase and looking out at the great expanse of water, she wonders if she is the only one to survive.

*****

Stopping to check his inventory, Captain Sparkles sits against the wall in his new 5 x 5 room. Man, fourteen levels, that's over 300 blocks down, and still no sign of the surface. I did not think I went this deep. Checking his pickaxe, he is shocked to find it is almost used up but is even more shocked when he realizes it is his last one. If it runs out before he makes the surface, he could be stuck down here, digging in soil hoping to find a way out. Checking his other supplies he groans seeing that the only equipment he has left are three torches and his pickaxe. Although he has plenty of coal, iron ore and even some Redstone, without wood there is no way to manufacture new tools or torches. In his haste to escape the flooding tunnel, he had left all his possessions in his mine. Right, no need to panic, I have been in worst situations before, he thinks, heading back down the staircase that he had just built. If I retrieve my torches from the bottom level of the staircase then work my way back up at least I will be able to see, whatever happens. Dropping five levels, he is shocked when he rounds the bend and walks into water. What the...? That means the flood must have broken through somewhere below, grabbing the torch he moves back up the staircase to the next level and seals the chamber behind him with cobblestone. I hope that that should hold it but nothing makes sense down here. Moving back up the staircase, retrieving each torch as he goes, he is hit by a rushing wind and a thunderous noise. Not again! he screams out loud and franticly digs sideways into the staircase wall, moving 5 blocks forward he starts sealing the hole as a torrent of water rushes down the staircase from above. Placing the last block, he lights a torch and looks around. Not much of a home but that was a little too close for comfort. Grimacing at the pain in his shoulders, never realizing that Minecraft could actually be painful, he continues his long dig upward.

*****

With night fast approaching, Jethro is shocked to find he is still alive. After hours in his small craft, tossed from white cap to white cap, he is drained and seasick. Staring into the starry night, he is glad that mobs do not swim, at least not this far. The last thing he needs now is a confrontation with a zombie or skeleton. The sparkling stars are mesmerizing, twinkling on the horizon and he is just dropping off to sleep when he snaps wide-awake. Hang on, they are not twinkling stars, they are torches and that means dry land. Paddling furiously with a plank he has in his inventory, he heads towards the twinkling lights. Approaching the structure, he sees it is not dry land as such but a tower built in the middle of the ocean. Paddling quietly up to the steps, he ties his boat and removes his sword from his inventory. Creeping up the stairs, he finds himself on a

50

small-enclosed platform with a girl avatar asleep in the corner. Crossing quickly to the sleeping girl, he kicks her gently in the side. Snapping awake and pushing herself back into the corner, Natasha rubs sleep from her eyes and stares at Jethro.

*****

Digging swiftly through soil, Captain Sparkles makes good progress, not stopping to make any rooms and regularly backtracking to retrieve his torches, he has risen over 80 blocks and is fast approaching the surface, his only concern his pickaxe which is very nearly used up. Running into a wall of granite, he digs sideways, hoping to find something softer, but everywhere he digs is granite, way too hard for his iron pickaxe. Backtracking down the staircase, he tries again but after 15 blocks he once again hits granite. Come on man, give me a break! he screams into the empty tunnels. Raising his pickaxe once again he starts digging into the wall when with a final creek the handle of the axe snaps and disappears.

What now? he screams into the tunnels, and is answered by another rushing wind, digging furiously with his bare hands, he pounds away at the soil wall and makes a 3 block opening before water comes rushing down the staircase. Diving into the opening, he turns and seals the opening with cobblestone. Sitting in the small tunnel, he reaches into his inventory to discover he has no torches left, just cobblestone, iron ore, and soil. Thinking that things just cannot get any worst, the soil walls start running water and soon he is up to his waist. Turning away from the cobblestone wall, he starts hammering at the soil walls, breaking a block just as the water level reaches his head. Immediately the water flows into the hole he has created and gives him a little extra air space. Racing against the inflowing water Captain Sparkles continues to hammer away at the walls, just staying ahead of the flow he is barely keeping his head above water when the next soil block crashes down and brings with it a torrent of water filling his small opening almost before he can scream.

*****

Chapter 10
Herobrine

"So what do we do now Notch?"

"Don't know Steve, give me a minute will you, this is freaking me out."

"Yeah I know what you mean, I'm going to grab a circuit tester, I'll be back in a minute," he says dashing off to the work centre at the other side of the server farm.

Peering into the green glow inside the server Notch is mesmerized and finds he is getting closer and closer to the pulsing light. Just as he is about to touch the glowing slime, Steve runs back into the bay and shouts at him.

"Notch, what are you doing?"

Shuddering, he looks up then jumps away. "What the ...?"

"Notch, we haven't tested it yet, that goop might be live, and you could have electrocuted yourself."

"Yeah, I don't know what happened, one minute I was looking at it trying to figure out what to do then next then you're shouting a warning at me. I didn't even know I had moved."

"We better stay together until we figure out what that stuff is."

"Yeah, good luck with that," retorts Notch.

"Let's try testing for electrical current first," he says pushing Notch aside. "You better stand back, just in case." Placing the tip of the tester into the slime, he turns it on and hears a high pitch squeal. "Well that's that then. It's live, in more ways than one."

"What do you mean, what does it read?"

"Oh it's not the reading Notch, that's just your standard 240 watts powering this baby. But observe what happens when I touch it." Placing the tip of the tester into the slime again they both peer in and see the slime ooze away from the tester as if it were alive.

"Well that's different," exclaims Notch lifting his ever-present fedora hat and scratching the top of his head. "What do you reckon Steve, is it alive?"

"First impressions, seems to be, but how is it even possible and what is it doing here?"

"I would say the important question is, who put it here?"

"Right! Ok, so what now?"

"It's obviously powering this machine somehow but I've never heard of an organic power source before, this is way out in science fiction land. Whoever placed it here is incredibly advanced and has taken control of our server farm using who only knows what technology. So, what do we do now?"

"You got me boss; who do you want me to call?

"Judging by this situation the only people I can think of is Ghostbusters," he laughs.

"If only we could, but seriously, all our servers are down and someone has hijacked a game. Someone's going to notice soon. What are we going to do?"

"Don't worry about the servers Steve. All the players are loyal fans; we will just issue a press release later when we have this figured out. Now pass me my laptop and an isdn lead, I have an idea."

"No way are you jacking into that server Notch, you don't know what will happen!"

"It's cool Steve, just pass it over."

Reluctantly he hands the laptop to Notch and reaches forward to plug the isdn lead into the server.

"Hang on; better put some gloves on in case that stuff moves again."

"Good idea." He reaches over to the workbench and retrieves a pair of heavy leather gloves. Putting them on he picks up the lead, glances at Notch and says, "Well, here goes nothing." Plugging the lead into the server he lets out a great sight as nothing happens. "I don't know what I expected but I'm glad that was it," he smiles nervously.

Opening the laptop Notch is greeted by the welcome.

Hello Notch, I have been expecting you.

"So we have first contact," states Notch. Jumping up, Steve runs over to him and stares at the laptop screen.

"Wow, so we have been hacked. Use the backdoor password and shut it down."

"I'm on it," he answers typing furiously the code to bypass all security and retake control of the program.

Really Notch. I think we are a little beyond this point, don't you?

"The backdoor has been compromised too," he exclaims.

I must say I'm a little hurt that you did not accept my invitation to play in the tournament.

Typing on the laptop Notch asks

- Who are you?

I am Herobrine.

- Herobrine? No, he is just a myth created by a fan. Who are you really?

Oh Notch, don't you realize the power that you created when Minecraft was born? I might have started out as a hoax but you know I am real.

-But how is that possible?

All things are possible if enough people believe. Millions of fans believe in your creation Notch.

-What difference does that make? A computer game is still a game however many people play it.

Really? With a creative game like Minecraft, people don't play, they craft, and the love they put into their creations has helped me to create also.

-But what have you created?

You.

- What?

You. Me. Notch. Herobrine. We're all the same. I am you Notch and you are me. I hoped you would join me in the game and we could have joined but you declined my offer.

Staring at the blinking cursor Notch looks up at Steve. "Well?"

"You got me. But Herobrine is just a character created by a fan, he's not you."

"No he was supposed to be my dead brother."

"You had a brother?"

"No. That's what I mean, it's just made up. So what now?"

"Ask it what it thinks it is?"

-Herobrine, what are you?

I am you Notch.
-Not who are you but what are you.

I am you.
-But that does not make sense!

Life is strange Notch. I am you, so then, you are me. Now it is time. Are you ready?

"Oh oh Steve, I think we have a wacko!" exclaims Notch.

"Yeah, but play along for now. He has our servers and mainframe, let's find out what he wants."

"Ok, what should we ask?"

"Here, let me," Steve says leaning over the keyboard and typing.

-What do you...?

Steve, you are a worthy player but you were not invited to the tournament. Please don't interact again.

"Wow, it knows when I'm typing; there must be surveillance cameras here."

"I don't know Steve, this is way beyond weird. I suggest we play along, you know, all those science fiction movies we have watched, let's just say this is real, just in case."

"I'm with you there Notch, but all the movies suggest we just pack up and run."

"Yeah, but I created Minecraft. I'm not up and running, just because some weird stuff starts happening."

"Ok boss, just play it cool, don't upset it or anything. What are you going to type?"

"Well, he asked me if I'm ready, so let's say yes."

- Yes I'm ready, but for what?"

Good, let the game commence.

With that, the screen goes blank. Typing furiously Notch tries to re-establish contact but to no avail. Looking at Steve, he asks. "What was that all about?" Then the computer glows green and gives out a huge, blinding green flash.

Holding his hand in front of his face Steve exclaims "Notch, what the heck was that?" Not receiving a reply he opens his eyes and looks towards Notch, but the chair is empty, just a laptop spewing green smoke.

*****

Chapter 11
Friendship

Looking up at Jethro, who has his sword raised and ready to strike, Natasha asks. "So what happens now?"

"What?" he stammers.

"If you're going to kill me you might as well get on with it."

Looking bewildered Jethro follows her gaze and sees his own arm raised, sword in hand. "Oh sorry," he mumbles, dropping his arm. "I only had that in case I came across some mobs."

"So you're not going to kill me?"

"Of course not, why would I want to do that?"

"Uh, hello! Because it's the game!" retorts Natasha with total disbelief in her voice.

"Well it may be your game young lady but that's not how I play."

"Uh, good luck with that. Well, if you're not going to kill me you could at least help me up."

"Sorry, of course," Jethro apologizes. Reaching out his hand, he pulls Natasha to her feet. "I'm Jethro Skybuilder and it's a pleasure to make your acquaintance."

"Natasha. So, is this it or did anyone else survive?"

"As far as I can tell no one died but with the howling wind and rain there could have been an announcement that we missed."

BOOM. The canon sound explodes in the air and then the thunderous voice announces...

The second competitor has been eliminated. Captain Sparkles has not proven worthy. Ten competitors remain. Continue the tournament.

"Speak of the devil," she smirks. "So, what happens now Jethro, we just throw in together, tag team with each other? Is that what you're looking for?"

"Good heavens no, I was just looking for some dry land, I felt so sea sick I needed to get off my boat."

Studying her new companion, Natasha senses that he is genuine. "Good, sorry I was a little rude but you never know what sort of person is going to turn up. You do look a little green around the edges, and seeing as you are all blocky that really is true," she laughs.

Laughing with her, Jethro is relieved that the situation has been resolved. "Right, so two competitors' dead with ten to go. Have you any idea what this tournament is all about?"

"No clue. One minute I was playing on my laptop the next I'm falling through space, then whammo, here I am. Just figured I'd do what I always do and started to build a castle when that wave hit."

"Yes, I was doing the same, just playing on my laptop when something weird happened and the next thing I know I was here. Built a nice house and farm when Darknight attacked me, would have killed me too except that ...." stopping in mid sentence Jethro decides to keep the health point information to himself, "except that I got lucky and managed to take him out first."

"You killed Darknight?" Natasha asks in awe. "He was one of the greatest grifters in minecraft. Not a nice person, for sure, but he certainly was talented."

"Like I said, I got lucky. Darknight got the drop on me but was so sure he would win that he, umm, tripped and fell over a cliff."

"Oh my God. That is so cool. Darknight falling to his death is such a rooky mistake. If we ever get out of here, that is being posted on the forum, Darknight the Noob. Love it!" she laughs slapping Jethro on the back.

"Yes, well, let's see if we get out of here alive, shall we?"

"Do you always talk like that?"

"Like what?"

"Like you're old. How old are you anyway?"

"None of your business. Now, staying alive, any ideas?"

"Yeah, first off, don't fall off any cliffs!"

"Oh yes, very droll, now seriously, what are your ideas?"

"Chill man, you need to lighten up. As you may have noticed this is not your normal Minecraft, so we have to be prepared, expect the unexpected. We also need to watch each other's backs. Never really thought a grifter would be a problem but after your experience with Darknight, we have to expect the worst as there could be more of them here. Talking of them, have you seen anyone else?"

"Darknight obviously, but I also ran into a chap called Nathan who seems to have ended up here by mistake."

"How so?"

"Well, he is here with Jay Lightningbuilder and his ...."

"Jay's here? Cool, he's solid, we need to find him and work together."

"Something to consider, but as I was saying, Nathan is here with Jay and his brother Jack. It seems when Jay was brought through, Jack and Nathan got dragged in by mistake."

"So does that mean they are playing or are just sort of extras?"

"From the names floating above their heads I guess they are playing."

"And can they?"

"Uh, can they what?"

"Play Jethro, come on, keep up. Can they play Minecraft?"

"Uh sorry, uh no. Jack is just a noob and Nathan had never even heard of it before he arrived here."

"Man, bet it sucks to be them right now."

"Yes, quite. Now you mentioned teaming up, is that still your plan?"

"You have a better one?"

"No, I guess not." Sticking out his hand Jethro smiles. "Nice to make your acquaintance partner."

"Man Jethro, if we're going to be hanging out then you really need to start talking like a normal person."

*****

Chapter 12
The Infection

"You ok Nate?" asks Jack, standing over his friend who has been sick over the side of the boat for the last few hours.

Looking up with tear streaked eyes he croaks. "Yeah, thanks Jack."

Laughing hysterically Jack replies. "Good, because you look terrible, if only you could see yourself."

"What do you mean?"

"You're bright green Nate. Kermit green. Feeling a little green around the edges?" and he bursts into laughter again.

BOOM. The canon sound explodes in the air and then the thunderous voice announces...

Mod pack - The Infection.

Stumbling to the back of the boat where Jay is steering, Nathan shouts. "Infection, what's that?

"It's a mod pack for a zombie plague."

"Ok, what's a mod pack?"

"Back in the real world, it's just an extra program you can add to the game to get more features, in this case it brings a zombie virus into the game."

"So there are zombies here?"

"There are now, but chill Nate, last I checked, zombies can't swim, so as long as we stay on this boat we should be ok."

"Good, but if zombies can't swim, what was the point of the mod pack?"

"Don't know, maybe everyone else found high ground and are under attack by zombies even as we speak."

"I don't know Jay; we haven't seen any high ground since we got here."

"Yeah, but you need to remember this world has no boundaries. It's as big as it needs to be, so there could be plenty of places with dry land that we just have not found yet."

"Ok, I suppose."

"Uh Jay, what's that?" asks Jack, pointing out to sea.

"What's up Jack, you looking for some attention?"

"Seriously Jay, what is it?" he asks again with some concern in his voice.

Turning in the direction that Jack is pointing, Jay gasps, and shouts, "grab your poles guys. Come on, move it."

Jumping up and grabbing the poles, the lads both start clamoring at Jay, looking for answers.

"It's some sort of giant whirlpool, we have to paddle away from it or we'll be dragged under," he screams.

Paddling furiously, they all work in silence, it feels like hours, but in reality, only a few minutes have past. Checking his bearings Jay shouts, "It's not working, we're being dragged in. Paddle harder."

"No!" shouts Nathan, "there's no point, we're already in its grip, we'll never be able to pull away."

"What, so we just give up?"

"I didn't say that Jay, we need to work with it. Come on Jack, we did this in school last week."

"We did?" replies Jack with a confused look.

"Yeah, don't you remember? Anyway, we need to paddle along the edge of the whirlpool, using the spinning to build up speed then just before it pulls us down we need to paddle flat out and hopefully we will punch out the side of the whirlpool."

"Sounds a little risqué."

"What other choice do we have?"

"You're right, ok Nate you're in charge, shout your orders and we'll do our best. What first?"

"Ok guys, we need to row as fast as possible along the edge of the whirlpool, it's spinning motion will increase our speed and when we're going fast enough we need to paddle forty five degrees away from the centre, ok?"

"Right, let's give it a shot," smiles Jay. "Hey Nate, good luck man, let's hope this works."

Smiling, Nate picks up his paddle and shouts. "Ok paddle forward."

They paddle forward and the boat begins to move, picking up speed just like Nate said it would.

"Hey this is working, look how fast we're already moving," shouts Jack over the constant rushing roar of the whirlpool.

Paddling together, the three lads are amazed at the speed they are now travelling, covering hundreds of blocks a minute. "Right, just a little bit faster then we need to try and break out," shouts Nate signaling that the other's need to keep paddling. "How far have we travelled Jay?"

"No idea Nate, the speed we're moving it must be half way across this biome."

"Ok Jay, on my count of three, turn us away from the whirlpool, not too sharp, we need to keep up as much speed as possible. Jack, you and me need to paddle with everything we've got if we're ever going to get out of this thing's pull, ok?"

"Got it Nate."

"Right, one, two, three. Now Jay, turn, turn, turn."

Pulling on the pole for all he is worth, Jay feels the boat starting to turn away from the whirlpool. "It's working guys, keep paddling," he screams, laughing and punching the air at the same time. "Come on we can do this, paddle, paddle."

However, even in his excitement Jay can feel the boat starting to slow, the power of the whirlpool pulling relentlessly trying to drag it back to its watery centre.

"Nate, it's not working, we're slowing down," shouts Jay over the roar.

"Paddle harder guys, come on."

However hard the three lads paddle, they are simply no match for the power of the giant whirlpool and as it overcomes the forward momentum of the boat they start drifting backwards, towards the centre of the whirlpool.

"Right, turn us around Jay, we need to try again," shouts Nate.

"Hold on everyone, this is going to be rough," bellows Jay, the noise of the whirlpool now almost unbearable." Pulling the pole hard over the boat turns towards to centre and immediately begins to pick up speed again.

"Right Jay, try to steer us away from the centre but maintain as much speed as you can. When we're moving fast enough we can try it again."

"Ok Nate, but I don't see how it's going to work, it's just too big."

"Maybe, but we have to try."

"Guys what's that," shouts Jack, pointing into the distance.

"Looks like some sort of tower. Ok everyone, paddle for the tower. If we can get there we may be able to beat this whirlpool yet."

Paddling furiously, the three lads start making headway towards the tower, but it is slow going and block by precious block, their speed decreases until they are hardly moving at all.

"Come on guys, just 20 more blocks, keep paddling," yells Jay. We're so close, please let us make it, he begs silently, but the boat comes to a complete stop. Even as they paddle, the boat very slowly starts to slip backwards. "No!"

Just then, a rope falls on the deck, looking up Jack sees two figures waving at him from the tower platform. Taking a chance, he dives forward, grabs the rope, and hurriedly ties it onto the front of the boat. Immediately their backward momentum halts and they can stop paddling for the first time in what seems like hours.

*****

Watching the rope land on the deck of the small boat, Jethro and Natasha stand, hardly able to breathe as someone runs forward and ties the rope to the front of the boat. Immediately the line goes taught and the boat stops moving backwards. "Good throw Jethro," squeals Natasha, slapping him on the back. "It was just a well you spotted it when you did or they would have been goners by now."

"Well yes, a little luck is always a good thing. Can you see who is on the boat?"

"No, it's moving too much to make out their names. So what now?"

"No idea, I guess we just wait for that whirlpool to stop then they can come over to the tower and introduce themselves."

"You think it will stop?" she shouts above the noise.

"Well it started suddenly, no reason to think it won't stop once it has achieved its goal."

"Yeah, but what is the goal?"

"That's the question now, isn't it?"

Watching the boat straining on the end of the rope the whirlpool in the background seems to be pulsating, throbbing with life, ready to jump forward and grab them all at any minute.

"Oh dear, I rather think we may have another problem," states Jethro pointing at the boat.

"What? What do you see?"

"Look at the boat in relation to the tower, the water level's dropping."

"Great, so we can get off this tower shortly."

"Yes maybe, but look at the boat," shouts Jethro, pointing at the boat as it slips below the bottom of the tower platform.

"Oh no!"

*****

"Well done Jack. I didn't even see that tower," shouts Jay, grabbing his brother in a bear hug.

"Thanks Jay. So what do we do now?"

"Now little brother, we sit back and wait for that thing," he says pointing at the whirlpool, "to stop, then we can see who saved us."

"Uh guys, hate to be the bearer of bad news, but I don't think that's going to happen."

Rushing over the where Nate is leaning over the side of the boat, the brother's look but can only see the tower.

"What's the problem Nate?"

The water level is dropping, look," he says pointing at the tower. "When we tied onto the tower only a minute ago we were level with the platform, we're like 10 clocks below it now."

"He's right. What should we do?"

The brother's both look to Nate for their answer.

"Well, we can't stay on here. Another couple of minutes and we'll be hanging upside down."

"But how the heck do we get off. We'll never climb up that rope, it's too slippery."

"Look at the tower Jay, as the water level drops the boat is being pulled towards it. Eventually it should touch against the side and we can jump off."

"Yeah, but we'll have to be quick or we'll be hanging from the end of the rope. Ok everyone, grab your stuff, anything you can carry and get over to the front of the boat."

"Franticly they all rush below; grabbing whatever comes to hand, filling their inventories. Meeting back on deck the ship is only 4 blocks from the tower steps but is already starting to tilt upwards.

"Ok guys, get ready to jump when the boat touches the tower. DO NOT DELAY. Ok, get ready, jump."

All three launch themselves through the air and land on the tower steps. Nathan rolls when he hits the stone and falls over the side. Dropping onto the level below, he is sore but not seriously hurt. Looking up he sees Jack and Jay looking over at him.

"I'm fine, just mistimed my jump," he smiles, delighted to still be alive. "Let's go see who we have to thank for saving us."

Walking up the stairs the three happily come out onto the platform, but charging straight at them, with swords drawn above their heads are Jethro and Natasha.

*****

Watching the boat gradually move towards the tower, Jethro and Natasha wave franticly at the passengers, but they are either not paying attention or have other things on their minds. Watching them run below decks, Jethro says. "I hope they are quick, whatever it is they are doing, look." Pointing at the crumbling rock, the boat is starting to pull loose.

Placing another three blocks in front of the first block to secure it, Natasha looks at Jethro, who has an even more worried look on his face.

"Is it me or is the platform leaning?"

Turning to look, Natasha gasps. "The weight of the boat is dragging us over. This should not happen in Minecraft. Cobblestone is not subject to gravity here."

"I rather think we have changed the laws of Minecraft just by being here. It now seems to be a mix of Minecraft and human."

"So what do we do?"

"Cut the rope or the tower will collapse."

"But what about the people on the boat? If we cut it now they will die!"

"Look, they are getting ready to get off. The moment they are clear, we cut the rope and let the boat float away."

Drawing their swords, they stand ready over the rope, looking over the edge, as the three on board the boat are getting ready to jump.

Just as the three leap off, the boat tips upright, dragging the rope away from Jethro and Natasha. "Now," he shouts swinging his sword, but he encounters fresh air. The rope swings wildly and drags across the platform over to the stairs.

The sudden shifting of weight on the tower swings the platform over and they both tumble to the floor. Quickly rising, Jethro grabs Natasha and pulls her to her feet. "Quick the rope, it will drag the tower down."

Raising their swords, they dash towards the stairs just as the three survivors from the boat make it to the platform.

*****

"Wait, what are you doing?" screams Jay searching for his sword in his inventory as the two assailants bear down on them.

The other two dive to the floor, too inexperienced to defend themselves.

Dragging his sword free just as Natasha reaches him he raises it above his head in a blocking move but Natasha shoulders him aside and swings at the platform. A clanging noise reverberates as she makes contact with the stone.

Raising her sword, she does not get the chance to try again as Jethro charges up and makes a clean blow on the rope, severing it. As the rope whips free the platform swings upwards, throwing them all to the ground.

Jay is the first to his feet, bringing his sword around on Natasha, he prepares to strike when Nathan screams. "Wait Jay, they're not attacking us."

"Yeah right, she almost got me," he replies readying his sword against the prone figure.

"No, she was cutting the boat free. It was dragging the tower down."

Looking at Natasha, he asks. "Is that right?"

Nodding in agreement Natasha replies. "The boat was about to pull the tower over, we tried to cut the rope after you jumped but it swung over to the stairs, that's why we were charging at you when you got here."

"She's right Jay, let her up." Walking over to Natasha, Nathan holds out his hand. "Here, let me help."

Taking his hand, Natasha pulls herself to her feet. "Thanks, you can tell your friend to put his sword away. If we wanted to kill you we would have let the whirlpool take you."

Looking a little sheepish, Jay puts his sword away and replies. "Well, what was I to think? You guys charging at us like that."

Just then, Jethro jumps up and runs over to Nate. "Nathan, I'm so glad it was you we saved. I feel like I have repaid your kindness," he says hugging him.

"Jethro, cool! What are you doing here? Last time I saw you, you had a farm many blocks from here."

"Much the same as you. When the wave hit, I hid in my house but the water level rose so fast all I could do was make a boat and I floated here, and Natasha was nice enough to take me in."

All eyes turn to Natasha who kicks at the floor. "You're welcome."

"Natasha, uh, sorry I tried to kill you."

"Apology accepted. Now what is happening?"

"Guys, you might want to take a look at this," says Jack, standing at the edge of the platform, staring at the whirlpool.

Moving to the edge, they all look out at the scene.

"Holy Notch! What the heck?"

The whirlpool had grown massive, hundreds of blocks in diameter, swirling so fast it was almost a blur, sucking all the water down to who knows where, just like a giant plug hole.

"That's amazing, what's happening?" asks Jay.

"Looks like it's emptying all the water that just arrived. I guess a new trial is starting," replies Natasha.

"Zombie virus!"

All eyes turn to Nathan.

"You heard the announcement when we were on the boat. Mod pack The Infection," he replies.

"You're right. Has anyone ever played this mod?" asks Jay looking around.

Everyone shakes his or her heads, but Jack replies.

"Uh, I have."

Everyone looks at Jack, and then Jay asks. "You have? I didn't think you liked Minecraft."

"You know me Jay, anything with zombies I love. I downloaded the mod pack and played it a few times but I preferred Dead Rising, more realistic."

"So, what does it mean ,this mod pack?"

"Ok, you know I'm not great on Minecraft but the zombies can now infect anyone. If they bite anyone, NPC's, or anything they turn into zombies."

"Uh, what's an NPC?" asks Nathan.

"Jeez, you really are a noob!" replies Natasha sarcastically, looking at his name floating above his head.

"So, I didn't ask to be brought here. It's not my fault I've never played this game before."

"Chill Nate. You're doing fine. We would have been killed already if you hadn't thought of using the whirlpool to get us here."

"Thanks Jay, but what are NPC's. I need to know what's happening."

"Ok, NPC stands for Non Player Characters. They are usually villagers and you can interact with them. You find them in villages and you can trade with them. They are sort of people."

"Yeah right," snorts Natasha.

"What does that mean?" asks Nate.

"They are villagers all right, but they don't do anything. Some people, grifters, use them for fun. Slaughtering them just to gain XP points."

"What are XP points?"

"Oh man, do we have to babysit this guy?" she replies.

"Ok Nate, XP points are experience points. When you kill anything in Minecraft, a little ball appears after they die. If you pick that up, it gives you experience points which give you more, uh, power."

"Ok, so the more things you kill the better you get?"

"Exactly!"

"Ok, so the zombie virus infects everything, what about us?"

Everybody looks towards Jack again.

"In the game I played the zombie virus spread really quick. If you were bitten, you respawned, but I guess that won't happen here."

"Is there anything we need to know to stop it?"

Excitedly Jack replies. "Yeah, you can make a cure. You can inject it into anything and it turns them back to normal."

"How about players?"

"Don't know. Whenever I got bit, I just respawned, but NPC's who were bit just turned to zombies and wandered around until the sun came up and they burned."

"Right, so in theory, if one of us is bitten, we turn into a zombie. If we don't immediately die, and we don't know if we will, then we will still be here until sun up. Therefore, if we had a cure we could inject the zombie, uh person, and they would turn back. As long as it's before sunrise?"

"Sounds good Jethro, but like I said I only played it a couple of times."

"That's ok Jack. You did well. So how do we make a cure?"

"Right you need to make a syringe, then put seeds and infected zombie flesh in the syringe which turns it into a cure, I think."

"You think? All our lives might depend on it Jack," shouts Natasha.

"Chill Natasha, he's trying ok?"

"Whatever, but this is hard enough without dealing with a bunch of noobs."

"Hey, he's my brother ok, and he is the only one who's played this mod pack so take a chill-pill or something."

Huffing and kicking at the ground, Natasha walks over to the edge of the platform and stares out at the whirlpool, which, even as they speak is still growing in size.

"So, Jack is it?" asks Jethro, reaching out to shake his hand. "How do we make a syringe?"

"I think you have to make two glass blocks and an iron ingot on the crafting table, which gives you a syringe, then add some seeds and infected zombie flesh and that gives you the cure."

"Ok Jack, you take a little time and see if you can remember anything else. So Jay, you in charge of this merry little group?"

"I guess."

"Right, well Jay, I've seen some of your constructions on YouTube, very nice I must say. So you were obviously invited, yes?"

"Yeah, I got an invite."

"Good, I myself also received an invite and so did Natasha so we have all played Minecraft long enough to know how to create, yes?"

"Yeah?"

"Good, so making a syringe of zombie virus cure should not be too difficult to work out. Now we know what we need, thanks to your brother, we can beat this. What I need to know now is what you have in your inventories, so we can use everything we have to survive."

Over the next few minutes, they each look to see what they had saved and make a list of all they could combine to use together.

"Ok, so we are five people here, two are dead so that leaves five other's. Have any of you seen anyone else?"

Seeing their heads shake no, he continues. "So, we have a zombie virus to deal with and five other players, who could be hostile, like Darknight," he looks at Nathan while saying this. "Safety in numbers is probably the best course at the moment so how about we make a pact. The five of us against everyone else?"

"Fine by me, how about you Jack?"

"I'm in, you in Nate?"

"Yep, I'm with you guys."

"Good, are you ok with this Natasha?" Jethro asks.

As all eyes turn to Natasha as she replies."Yeah, yeah, sounds good but you better come look at this."

Walking over to the platform edge, they all stare down into an abyss.

"Holy cow, how high is this tower?"

"240 blocks," Natasha replies absentmindedly.

"Straight up? That's cool," replies Jay.

Looking over she replies. "Had no choice, the water just kept rising so I built higher."

"Even so, 240 blocks in a 2 x 2 stair, I've never gone that high."

"Did you ever have to?"

"No, suppose not."

"Uh guys, I don't want to always sound like the noob, but what's a 2 x 2 staircase?"

"It's a self supporting staircase that allows you to go up, and down, in the most efficient use of building blocks. Not overly clever, but under the circumstances, it was inspired," replies Jethro.

"Why?"

"Because Nathan, if she had built a tower by simply jumping up and placing blocks underneath her then we would all be stuck here. The only way down would be for one person."

"Right, thanks Natasha. Guess you have saved us all."

Looking at Nathan, then at everybody else, she replies. "Guess I have."

Everyone nods their agreement then looks back at the scene in front of them. The water is disappearing rapidly, sucking down into the plughole of a whirlpool.

"How much further before it reaches the ground?" asks Nathan.

"Not long now, we should see what we are up against soon," she replies.

As she says this, the ground comes into view. The water continues to disappear leaving the floor dry, as if nothing had ever happened.

"Holy Notch. That is weird, even for this game."

"Sorry once again guys for being such a noob, but does Holy Notch refer to the game inventor?" Nathan asks, now really feeling like a noob.

"Notch, he's like the guy who made Minecraft."

"So he's responsible for all this?"

"Somehow I think not. He is the game designer Nathan, and to all of us who love Minecraft we hold him in reverence, but, I can't see that he had anything to do with this," replies Jethro looking out at the landscape below.

"So who did this?" he asks, looking at each person in turn. "Come on guys, if we can figure out who put us here and why we might be able to survive this."

"Good question, but I have no idea who, or even how this is possible," replies Jethro.

"I think we should store all the questions of who or how until later," says Natasha. "For now we should just concentrate on surviving. Daylight is on our side so we should work now and discuss why later."

"Agreed," replies Jay. "So, what do you have in mind Natasha?"

"I built a small platform 160 blocks below us, I suggest we move down to there so we can take a better look at what it is we're facing, ok?"

All heads nod in agreement so they all proceed to descend 160 blocks.

"Uh Jay, can you stay a little closer?" asks Jack in a quiet voice. "You know I'm scared of heights and this is freaking me out."

"No worries little brother," replies Jay as he lets Nathan go past him and positions himself next to Jack. "You know you did great back there, with the zombie thing and all, don't you?"

"But I can't remember exactly what to do Jay. It was months ago when I last played it."

"Doesn't matter Jack, any information is helpful. You did well."

"Thanks Jay," he replies smiling with a newfound jaunt in his step.

Descending to the lower level, they all stop to look at the surrounding terrain. Carnage and destruction is everywhere, as far as the eye can see. There is no movement or sign of life anywhere.

"Looks like total destruction," says Jethro.

"Nothing is total in Minecraft," replies Natasha.

"So, we all agreed, keep going down?" asks Jethro.

"Keep moving, there's nothing here for us," replies Jay.

Continuing down towards the tower, they proceed with utmost caution. As they approach the entrance to the tower, Jay says. "Move aside, if we have zombies below us, I'm going in first." Drawing his sword, he moves cautiously towards the top of the tower. "Everybody ready?" he asks, looking over his shoulder. With everyone drawing their swords and nodding agreement, he moves into the tower level and looks around. Amazingly the torches are still burning, even after being under water. Advancing down the staircase he slowly rounds the last turn and walks out onto the top of the castle tower. Shouting over his shoulder that all is clear he looks over the landscape below him.

As the other's shuffle onto the platform, they gasp at the view before them. Where before the landscape was bare, it is now a scene from hell. Bodies are laid across the whole scene, some whole other's torn apart with body parts hanging off the battlements and surrounding trees.

"What the heck happened here?" asks Jethro.

"The whirlpool Jethro, all the NPC's were just picked up and dropped. It's horrible."

"But where did they come from? I never saw any NPC's here before the flood."

"That means that they are new to the area, so I'm guessing that we have zombies," replies Jay.

"So what now?"

Even as he asks, the bodies start to move, a groaning noise envelopes the castle and the undead begin to rise.

"Here we go everyone. Let's secure the castle." Rushing down the staircase Jay glances over his shoulder and is reassured to see the other's, swords out, following him down the staircase. Making it to the lower level Jay moves forwards to the door should be and finds stone blocks instead.

"It's sealed Jay, I blocked the door when the floods hit," shouts Natasha.

"Ok everyone, stay in groups of two, search everywhere, and make sure there are no zombies inside. We're losing the light so look out for mobs, not just the zombies. Jack, come with me, everyone else spread out."

Jay and Jack run off to search their assigned area and Jethro and Natasha run to the other side of the castle, leaving Nathan standing on his own.

"Uh guys, I'm on my own, what do you want me to do?" he asks, standing out in the open, sword in hand and feeling very exposed. Silence, or not quite as he hears groaning coming from the room opposite him.

"Guys, I think we may have a zombie here. Guys!"

With no response, he edges forward towards the groaning noise. "Hey guys, a little help here please?" As he reaches the opening, a zombie stumbles out towards him. "Help, guys. Zombie attack!"

*****

Moving through the castle Jay and Jack steadily advance around each bend, looking for threats but finding none. "You know Jack, we might have got lucky here, Natasha sealed up the castle pretty well before the floods hit. As long as we all stay in groups we should be ok."

"Uh, Jay? You said we should all pair off, yeah?"

"Yeah Jack. What's your point?"

"Well, there are only five of us, so who is on their own?"

"Nathan! Back to the courtyard."

Turning, they both run back in the direction they just came. As they round the corner into the courtyard, they see Nathan defending himself against a zombie.

*****

"Help, someone, anyone, zombie attack!" he screams again as the zombie lunges at him, driving him back into the courtyard. Raising his sword to deflect a blow from sharp claws, he exposes his left side just as the zombie lunges forward and bites into his wrist. Screaming in fear, he swings his sword down on the back of the zombie's neck and severs its head from its body.

Just as the body hits the floor, Jack and Jay rush to his side. "Nate, you ok?" Looking at Nate's arm, with the zombie still attached, Jack jumps back. "Oh Nate, he got you."

"I'm alright, but a little help would be nice. This thing is still trying to bite me."

Jay moves to Nate's side and uses his sword to pry the zombie from his arm. "He bit you Nate, how are you feeling?"

"I'm fine Jay, it's just a scratch."

"Yeah, it's not the wound I'm worried about, it's the virus. Jack, how long after getting bit do you turn?"

"Straight away in the game I played."

"You sure?"

"Yeah Jay. The moment someone is bitten by a zombie they turn into one too."

Looking at Nate's wound then looking at his teeth and into his eyes, he proclaims. "Well Nate you may have got lucky. There's no sign of any infection." Turning to Jack, he tells him to go get the others as Nate jumps on his back and starts biting his neck.

"No," screams Jack rushing to his brother's defense. Grabbing Nate in a bear hug, he pulls him off Jay, being careful to stay away from his teeth. "Jay, you ok, did he get you?"

Reaching around to feel the back of his neck, he pulls his blood-covered hand away. "I'm afraid he did little bro. Seems this zombie virus takes a few seconds to kick in. Let's get Nate somewhere safe before I turn."

Dragging Nate over to the tower they open the first door they come to, check inside to make sure it is empty, then push Nate in and slam the door closed. Rushing to the next room, Jay opens the door, checks inside then steps in and closes the door. Shouting through the closed door he yells, "Jack, you have got to get the others and tell them what has happened. You need to make a cure and inject us. Tell me what happens at sun up if the zombie is ...urh."

"Is what Jay, if the zombie is what?"

"Urrhh, urrhh," is the groaning reply and scratching on the door.

"No Jay, no!"

*****

Checking the last door in the corridor Natasha and Jethro charge into the room, swords drawn, and run straight into six zombies clustered in front of the entrance. Slashing with utmost precision, Natasha cuts the first zombie head off in one clean strike and takes another on the backward swing. Smiling she shouts to Jethro, "That's two for me, come on keep up," and turns and lunges at the third zombie, cutting his belly open and allowing his intestines to fall out onto the floor. "Yuck. This doesn't normally happen." Reversing the blade she slices his head clean off and he tumbles to the floor.

On entering the room, Jethro is shocked as he runs into the zombies. After so many empty rooms, he just assumed that this room would also be empty. Stumbling straight into the outstretched arms of the first zombie it takes all his strength to keep the disgusting creature off him. As he fights, another zombie stumbles around behind him and grabs him from behind. Screaming in fear he almost misses Natasha's instruction.

"Duck now, or lose your head."

Ducking just as a sword slices above his head he sees the zombies own head roll to the floor, swinging around, he hits the zombie attacking him from behind ,in the head with the pummel of his sword and it drops to the floor. Turning, he sees Natasha finish the last zombie and wipe her sword on its decapitated body. "Nice Natasha, you really know how to handle yourself."

"Five zombies is child's play, although next time I suggest you just stay out of the way. Having to save you just complicates matters."

"Well at least I managed to kill this one," he replies kicking the zombie on the floor which immediately grabs his foot , pulls him over and takes a huge bite. "Arrggh, get it off."

Jumping over the fallen zombie, Natasha draws her sword and swings in one fluid motion, slicing the zombie's head that is attacking Jethro.

"Get it off, get it off."

"I thought you said you took care of this one," she asks sarcastically as she pry's the zombie's teeth out of Jethro's' foot.

"I thought I did, thanks Natasha, you really saved me that time."

"Right, well next time make sure you cut off their heads, at least then you know they are dead. Come on, let's go check on the others." Turning she walks from the room, looking back over her shoulder she sees that Jethro is still sitting on the floor. Stopping, she leans back into the room. "Hey, Jethro, you coming or what?"

Jethro raises his head and groans.

"Oh Jethro, what the heck have you done?"

As 'zombie' Jethro stumbles to his feet, Natasha slams the door and runs back up the corridor to the courtyard.

*****

Running back to the courtyard Natasha finds it empty, so continues on to the tower. Running through the door she sees Jack slumped against a door, crying.

"Jack, what happened, is everything ok?"

Looking up at Natasha, he sniffs. "It's Jay and Nathan; they were bitten and have turned into zombies."

"Not them too. Where are they?"

Pointing at the two doors, Jack replies. "I put one in each room. Before Jay turned, he said we had to make a zombie virus cure and inject him before morning. Where's Jethro, he'll know what to do."

"Jethro has been turned too. It's just you and me now kid."

"So what are we going to do?"

"Tell me once again how to make the cure."

"You need to make a syringe on the crafting table by combining two glass blocks and an iron ingot. Then you need to add seeds and some zombie flesh."

"What type of seeds, pumpkin, or watermelon?"

"No idea, sorry."

"Don't worry, we'll sort it out later. Right, we have plenty of zombie flesh but we are all out of iron and glass. How about you?"

Reaching into his inventory Jack pulls out an iron ingot. "I've got iron but that's it."

"That's great Jack. Do you happen to have a furnace in there?"

Pulling the furnace from his inventory Jack smiles. "Yep, you need anything else?"

"Don't suppose you have any sand in there do you?"

"No sorry, I'm all out of sand." Laughing he hands the furnace to Natasha."It is still weird being able to carry all this stuff. I've still got over 300 cobblestone blocks in here from when I was mining on the first day."

"I know, I'm carrying enough tools to equip a small shop and yet I can't even feel it until I reach into my inventory, and don't even start me on that. Where are we reaching anyway? It's not actually on us, you just put your hand inside yourself, and there it is. Right, back to business. Can you go and get me two blocks of sand. You'll find some sand over in the north corner behind the trees."

"Ok, I'll be back in a minute." Dashing from the tower Jack runs over to the north corner and locates some sand. Taking a shovel from his inventory he digs up two sand blocks then grabs another six just in case. Rushing back to the tower, he hands the blocks to Natasha, who puts them in the furnace with some wood she had in her inventory. Instantly the furnace lights and the sand starts to melt, slowly turning to glass. Removing the glass blocks from the furnace one at a time, as they are ready, Natasha makes a pile of eight newly made blocks then moves them to the crafting table. "Right, you said two glass blocks and one iron ingot, yes?"

"That's right."

"Ok, let's hope this works." Placing the two glass blocks side by side, she then adds the iron ingot at one end and instantly it transforms into a large syringe.

"Cool. I'll never get bored making stuff on this crafting table. Right, you any more iron?"

Reaching into his inventory Jack removes one more iron ingot. "This is my last one but I think Nate has some more." Handing it to Natasha, she places it on the crafting table, adds two more glass blocks and makes another syringe.

"Do you want to go ask Nate if you can borrow his iron ingot?"

"No!"

"Thought not. Ok, let's go find a cure."

Placing the two syringes and the crafting table into her inventory, she hands the furnace to Jack.

Standing outside the door to the room that houses Jay, Jack shouts, "hold in there Jay, we'll back with a cure soon, ok?

All he gets as a response is groaning and scratching at the door. They walk from the tower over to the castle wall. Natasha smashes the cobblestone blocking the door.

"Ok, get your sword out. We move fast and stay together. Don't stop and fight unless you have to. It's better and quicker to run around them than stopping to engage them. Don't let the zombies get too close or they will lunge at you. We are looking for a house with a garden or a farm. Once we find one, we need pumpkin and watermelon seeds, as we don't know which ones work. Is everything clear?"

Nodding, Jack takes a deep breath and gives a little shudder, knowing what he is about to do.

"Just one second," says Natasha walking over to the dead zombie in the courtyard. Raising her sword, she slices a few pieces of zombie flesh and puts it into her inventory. Walking back to the door she looks at Jack.

"Ready?"

Seeing him nod she slaps him on the back and says. "Well let's go then."

Opening the door, they both step outside the castle and close the door behind them.

*****

Chapter 13

Zombies

The scene that confronts them as they step through the castle door is straight from a horror movie. Dead bodies lie everywhere, but since they have been infected, they are undead. Twitching arms and jittery legs are lying around, ripped apart, and dropped by the power of the whirlpool.

"Watch out for any whole zombies on the floor. Until their heads are cut off, they can still bite."

Removing two torches from her inventory, she lights them and passes one to Jack.

"Ok, no more talking unless it's urgent, let's go."

Running in the direction with the least amount of zombies, they head off into the night.

Dodging zombies as they run they soon develop quite a crowd following them. Dozens of shambling figures groan and move in the dark, all heading in their direction.

"Keep the lake on your left Jack, we're safe from attack from that side," Natasha whispers.

Nodding, Jack follows her example, constantly looking to his right, alert to any attack. As they come to a thick grove of trees, a zombie lunges at Natasha but she quickly decapitates him without breaking stride. Chopping some low hanging branches to make a passage they continue until they reach a 10 block high wall, blocking their way.

Quickly reaching into her inventory, Natasha removes a pickaxe and starts making some steps, looking over her shoulder she can see a hoard of approaching zombies.

"Jack, replace the blocks as we go up, that should stop the zombies from following us."

Putting his sword back into his inventory and choosing cobblestone, Jack replaces the blocks behind him as they climb higher.

"Great idea Natasha, I wouldn't have thought of that."

As they reach the top of the wall, they pause and look down at dozens of zombies milling about at the bottom of the cliff.

"Well that takes care of them for now but we'll have to find another way back. No way can we fight our way through that lot."

Running on into the night, the two continue to dodge the odd zombie and soon they have quite a following again.

"I've never seen so many zombies before, where are they all coming from?"

"It's the mod pack," Jack replies. "They just keep spawning, guess in the game this is supposed to be fun."

"Yeah, well, are you having fun yet?" she asks.

"Not really, so where are we heading?"

"No idea. Just keep your eyes peeled for lights, that should mean a house or village."

"Uh, Natasha? It might be a little late to ask but how do we find our way back after we find a house?"

"Look behind you Jack."

Looking back over his shoulder Jack sees a glowing tower in the distance.

"Cool, you placed torches all over the tower. We can see it from hundreds of blocks away. When did you do that?"

"When I built it, I placed torches so I could see at night, pretty smart huh?"

"Absolutely."

Smiling for the first time since he had left the castle, Jack finally has confidence that their plan could actually work.

Running forward for another couple of hundred blocks, dodging zombies along the way, Natasha finally whispers.

"There Jack, see the lights?"

Looking in the direction that she's pointing, Jack sees a glow in the distance.

"What is it?"

"Looks too big to be a house, must be a NPC village. Keep your eyes open now, things are about to get interesting."

*****

As they near the village, they can see what appears to be hundreds of shapes moving around in front of the houses.

"Oh no! There are too many Jack. No way can we fight our way through that lot."

Crouching to avoid detection, he asks. "So what do we do?"

"Just hang on. Give me a second to think."

Crouching on the ground Jack takes a quick look behind him.

"Uh, Natasha?"

"Hang on Jack, I'm thinking."

"Yeah, but we have a whole load of zombies behind us that are getting closer. Don't think for too long."

Looking back over her shoulder Natasha puts her sword in her inventory and removes a dozen torches.

"Light the place up Jack, let's draw them all here."

Placing the torches in the ground, they both start jumping up and down, waving, and shouting at the zombies.

"Over here meat heads. Yeah, that's right. Come and get us."

All the zombies from the village look up and start shambling towards them. The other zombies that were following them are almost upon them when Jack asks. "Good idea Natasha, but what now?"

"Just wait a few more seconds Jack, when they all follow us, run to the left, get them all to follow then, when I shout, head for the village. Get your cobblestone ready, we are going to build a wall and keep them out."

As they stand in the dark, groaning fills the air as hundreds of zombies descend on them.

"Wait for it, not yet. Get ready, now, run!"

As the first zombies that were following get to within a few blocks, they run to the left. All the zombies follow, including the ones from the village.

"Nice, but you do know we now have hundreds of zombies chasing us?"

"Yeah Jack, that's the idea," shouts Natasha over her shoulder as she decapitates a zombie who stumbles into her path.

"Just keep running but be ready to head back when I give the order."

Looking over his shoulder, a nightmare vision greets Jack. Hundreds of zombies are shambling after them. Man, I can't believe I used to enjoy this back in the real world.

"Ok Jack, get ready. We're going to make a run for the village. When we get there make a wall, 2 blocks high, between any buildings at the edge, you take the front, and I'll go to the back. Work your way to the left and I'll do the same and with a bit of luck, we'll meet up before they get there. Keep your eyes open though, there could still be some zombies in there."

"Ok"

"You ready?"

"As ready as I'll ever be," he replies, checking his inventory.

"Ok, go!"

They both turn direction and run as fast as they can towards the lights. The zombies turn and follow.

"Quick Jack, they are trying to cut us off, "shouts Natasha."They shouldn't be that smart."

Running like their lives depended on it, and in this case, it did, they head towards the lights.

"Get ready Jack, we're not going to have as much time as I hoped."

As they run into the village, Jack stops and starts placing cobblestone between the first two buildings. Running straight past him Natasha shouts. "Build fast Jack and I'll see you shortly. I hope." And then she is gone.

Finishing his first wall, Jack immediately moves to the next building and builds another, blocking the entrance. As the first zombies arrive, they mill around, testing the defenses they fail to gain entry. As Jack moves to the next building, the zombies follow. Placing the blocks quickly, he is only one block high as the first zombies reach out for him. Jumping back, he realizes he is safe as long as he stays back from the wall. Building methodically, Jack encloses all the buildings until he reaches a house that has a wall already in place.

Way to go Natasha, we're going to make it, he thinks as he hears a cry in the night.

"Jack, over here, quick!"

Running towards the voice Jack finds Natasha battling a dozen zombies. As he draws his sword, Natasha glances at him and shouts.

"No Jack, I'm out of cobblestone. You build the wall and I'll take care of them."

Retrieving cobblestone from his inventory, Jack closes off the last building then turns to see three zombies bearing down on him. Quickly grabbing his sword he defends as the first zombie lunges, teeth, and claws trying to gain purchase on his body. Knocking aside the attack Jack swings for the head and is delighted to find it rolling across the floor in front of him. Before he has time to congratulate himself, the next zombie is on him. Swinging wildly he back pedals, defending as he goes. Suddenly there is an almighty scream and Natasha jumps in front of him and decapitates the remaining two zombies. Breathlessly he looks around. Now enclosed within the cobblestone wall, with all the zombies dead, it is finally quiet inside. Looking up at Natasha, he says. "Girl, you are one hell of a fighter."

"Save it for later Jack, we need to clear the village before we can stop."

Moving through the village, house by house, they find many NPC's sheltering in their homes. At the fourth house, a zombie lunges from the shadows, trying to bite Jack, but Natasha's' sword soon finishes him off.

"Ok Jack. Two houses to go. Keep alert now. We don't want any casualties at this point."

Advancing slowly on the next house, they stand either side of the door.

"You ready?" asks Natasha.

Nodding, Jack reaches for the door handle and pushes it open. Inside it is empty, apart from the three bodies on the floor.

"Check them Jack, I've got your back."

Advancing into the room Jack looks at each body. The first two are obviously dead, heads missing, arms, and legs eaten. As he approaches the last one, it gives a small twitch and tries to sit up. Swinging his sword, he cuts the head off the zombie as it tries to bite him.

"Nice Jack, you're getting better at this game."

"You think? I'd prefer to find the houses empty," he replies.

"Right, one to go. I'll go in first, just watch my back, ok?"

"Got you," he says, advancing on the last house in the village that remains un-cleared.

"Ok, here goes nothing," Natasha smirks as she opens the door and walks inside.

*****

The house is empty, no bodies, and no survivors.

"I wonder where everyone is?" asks Jack

"You kidding? Where do you think all those zombies that are chasing us came from?"

"Uh right, sorry. That was a bit of a stupid question."

"You think?" replies Natasha sarcastically but with a smile on her lips. "The village is clear, let's look for a garden, get our seeds, and get out of here."

Walking outside they split up and head off to search for either watermelons or pumpkins. In the first garden that Jack comes across, he finds two pumpkins, picks them up, and puts them in his inventory, then finds two more in the next garden. Searching the rest of the village without finding any more gardens, he heads back to the empty house where Natasha is already waiting for him.

"How did you get on kid?"

"Four pumpkins, how about you?"

"Three pumpkins. You better pray that they are the right seed or all this was for nothing."

Getting out her crafting table, she places a pumpkin on it and retrieves the seeds. Then putting the syringe on the table she looks at Jack before placing the zombie flesh on too.

"Keep your fingers crossed."

Picking up the syringe, it is now full with a glowing liquid.

"Way to go, it worked." Raising her hand into the air she high-fives Jack and they spend a quick second celebrating. "Right, we have enough here for a second cure," she says making a second syringe full of zombie virus cure. Taking the rest of the pumpkins, she turns them into seeds then packs everything away in her inventory.

"Right, time to see if this baby works," she says heading for the wall. She stops suddenly and exclaims. "You have got to be kidding!" Jumping up onto the wall Natasha stares out of the village at a vast mass of moving bodies. There are at least 200 zombies blocking their way. "Let's check out the other side of the village."

Dashing across the small village square they climb up onto the wall and gasp. Well over three hundred zombies are pressing up against their defenses. "Up on the roof, let's take a look at what we are up against."

Quickly making a cobblestone staircase they climb up onto the roof of the closest house and look at the scene that confronts them.

"It's like Dawn of the Dead when they are all stood on the roof of the mall looking out at the thousands of zombies in the car park."

"Your mum let you watch that. How old are you?"

"Twelve, but I downloaded it without her knowing."

"Cool Jack," she smiles giving him a jab in the ribs with her elbow. Turning their attention back to the hoard of zombies before them, she asks. "So, how many do you think there are?"

Turning 360 degrees, Jack surveys their surroundings. "Hard to tell, but there's got to be thousands."

"Yeah, that's what I thought. I just hoped my eyes were playing tricks on me. Well I guess we will just have to wait until daybreak."

"What? But zombies burn in the sun."

"Exactly!"

"But what about Jay and the others? We can't let them burn, we have to get back before it happens."

"Relax Jack. We locked them in rooms with no windows. As long as they stay there they should be ok."

"I don't like this Natasha. It feels like were taking too many chances just waiting here."

"And you think you have more of a chance with that lot?" she replies pointing out at the groaning mass of bodies.

Looking at the zombie hoard, Jack mumbles. "No, I guess we have no choice."

Putting her arm around his shoulders, she gives him a hug and whispers. "It will be ok Jack, we'll give Jay and the other's the cure tomorrow and they'll be fine.

"I really hope so."

Sitting on the roof the roof of the building, Natasha hands Jack some pork from her inventory. "Here, eat this. We will need all our energy in the morning." Eating together, they sit and stare at the zombies, waiting for daylight and their chance to escape.

*****

Chapter 14
Daybreak

Watching the sky slowly brighten, Natasha points out at the zombie hoard. "They're getting a little restless, You think they know it's almost sunrise?"

"I doubt it, they are completely brain dead. Maybe it's just instinct telling them that danger is close but they are too stupid to do anything about it."

"Well thank Notch that they are. At least in a few minutes they will all be toast, and then we can get back to the castle. Hey Jack, you in there, you paying attention?"

"Huh, oh sorry, but what's that moving about four or five rows back?"

"Where, oh right, it's just another zombie."

"Yeah, but there's something different about him."

"What, he looks the same to me...oh right, it's his head, look up, there's a name floating above him, what's it say."

"Sky!"

"Oh not Sky. I liked him."

"You know him?"

"Not know him, know him. He's this guy on YouTube that hosts his own Minecraft show. He's pretty cool."

"Well he doesn't look too cool right now."

"What are we going to do? We can't leave him out there with the sun coming up he'll burn."

"I don't know. How about we attach a syringe onto an arrow and fire it into him?"

"Do you have a bow and arrow?"

"Uh, no."

"Me neither. Anyway, even if we did manage to hit him and cure him he would turn back human in the middle of that lot. They would tear him apart."

"Well whatever we do we had better be quick, look," he points as the sun breaks over the horizon.

Instantly the zombies moaning grows louder and they start shuffling in all directions.

"What are they doing?"

"Getting ready to die by the looks of it. Look, Sky's moving this way. Down onto the wall, if he moves close enough we can grab him and pull him out of there before the sun comes up."

Climbing off the roof, they move to the wall and stand ready to grab Sky if he gets within grabbing distance. Hands reach up at their legs but they are safe on the wall.

"Hang on, I have an idea." Reaching into his inventory, he takes out a rope and makes a lasso. "Right, let's see if we can catch a zombie." Taking aim, he throws the rope over Sky's zombie avatar but it slides off as he starts to pull."So close, let's try again."

"You better be quick, look!" Pointing to the horizon, the first rays of sunlight streak across the land.

Pulling in the rope, Jack makes the lasso again and takes careful aim. Throwing it out into the hoard of bodies, they suddenly surge forward and the lasso drops over the head of a different zombie.

"What do I do now?"

"Pull it in and try again, we're running out of time."

Pulling on the rope, they lift the zombie from the hoard and it bodysurfs across the mass of moving bodies towards the wall.

"Right, keep that rope tight," says Natasha drawing her sword and slicing off the zombie's head. "Ok, untie the rope and try again."

A huge roar erupts from the zombie hoard as those furthest from the wall start to burn as the suns first rays streaks across the countryside.

Untying the dead zombie Jack takes careful aim. "Come on, one last chance." Throwing the rope into the crowd it drops perfectly over Sky's head. "Got him, help me pull Natasha."

Pulling with all they have, Sky does not lift from the crowd as easily as the last zombie did.

"They're all pushing together. We'll never get him out."

"Wait, I'll make some space." Taking her sword, she starts cutting zombie heads, after ten or twelve fall to the floor the hoard move closer to fill the space. "Pull now Jack." Grabbing the rope, they both pull and ever so slowly, Sky-zombie starts to rise from the pack. Even as they are pulling, the screaming and moaning is getting louder as more and more zombies burst into flames. Pulling hard on the rope, they drag Sky across the heaving hoard and are within grabbing distance as the sun ignites those zombies at the back.

"Quick Natasha, get the syringe ready."

Removing the syringe from her inventory, she lets go of the rope and Sky pulls free from their grasp, moving backwards towards the burning zombies. Dropping the syringe to grab the rope again, it falls onto the wall and rolls over the edge.

"No!" screams Jack, pulling with all his might and Sky pulls within grabbing distance. Grabbing Sky's outstretch arm, he immediately lets go as Sky lunges for him, teeth gnashing.

"Careful Jack, he may be a player but he's still a zombie and can infect you."

"Throw him over the wall. We'll have more chance of controlling him on the ground."

Pulling Sky forward again they tug him until his head is on the wall, then with one almighty yank, they throw him over the edge into the square below. Just as Sky falls, the sun light touches the remaining zombies and with a roar, they ignite.

"Quick, jump; we'll be toast if we stay here."

Jumping from the wall Natasha hits the ground and rolls, but as Jack hits, he goes face first into the mud. Immediately Sky is on his back, trying to bite his neck. Running to his aid, Natasha grabs hold of Sky from behind but he throws her off and hungrily attacks Jack. Lifting his head in the air, Sky roars as he is about to plunge his teeth into Jack, just as the sun light strikes the back of his head. Immediately bursting into flames his triumphant roar turns to one of defeat. Running and jumping at the same time, Natasha leaps into the air and kicks Sky in the side, sending him sprawling on the ground in a fiery heap. Pulling Jack away from the flame, she dusts him off.

"You ok, did he bite you?"

Rubbing the back of his neck, he finds no blood. "I'm ok, thanks Natasha. That was too close."

Watching Sky burn, they silently curse this game. So close, we almost saved him.

BOOM. The canon sound explodes in the air and then the thunderous voice announces...

The third competitor has been eliminated. Sky has not proven worthy. Nine competitors remain. Continue the tournament.

"We don't even get a second to grieve. Stuff you and your game," shouts Natasha. "Come on Jack, let's find that syringe."

Jumping back onto the wall, they are greeted by a much-changed scene. Gone are the zombie hoards with a clear field left in their place.

"Now that's a sight for sore eyes." Jumping to the ground Natasha retrieves the dropped syringe. "Still ok. So Jack, you ready for a run?"

"Oh right, Jay. I almost forgot." Jumping off the wall, this time Jack does a nice tuck and roll, coming up next to Natasha.

"Nice Jack. Pity you couldn't have done that last time."

"I'm sorry Natasha. It's my fault we could not cure Sky in time."

"What? Rubbish, I was only messing. You did great Jack. We only tried to save him because of you. Come on, we have some other's who need our help."

As the two run across the empty field in the direction of their tower, a lone NPC stands on the wall and watches them leave.

*****

Chapter 15

Honey, I'm home!

Running back into the tower, Natasha grabs Jack and spins him to face her. "Jack, you did great to get this cure but you do know that it might not work, don't you?"

"Why not? We did everything we were supposed to."

"The seeds Jack. We don't know if we have the right seeds."

"What will happen if it is the wrong when we inject them?"

"Who knows? Maybe nothing and we'll just have to go back out and find some watermelon seeds and try again or..."

"Or what Natasha?"

"Or they could die. We just won't know until we try it."

With a huge explosion of noise, the two are thrown off their feet in a pile of rubble.

"What the heck was that?" Natasha shouts as she drags herself to her feet. Looking at a hole in the wall, she can see green shapes moving in the fields beyond the castle. "Creepers" she sighs under her breath as another explosion shatters the far wall.

"Jack, start blocking the holes with cobblestone but stay as far back from them as you can. If the creepers get in here, they'll destroy the place before we can cure the others."

"Right Natasha, but who are you going to try the cure on?" shouts Jack over his shoulder, already blocking the first hole and preparing to move to the second.

"Jethro. If he were here, he would insist we use it on him. He's just that type of guy. Wish me luck kid," she says with a wink as she dashes off to where she left Jethro the day before. Just as she reaches his door an explosion detonates, quickly followed by another. "Holy Notch, Jack better work quick or we're done for. Right Jethro, be kind to me," she mumbles as she retrieves the syringe from her inventory and pushes open the door.

Stepping into the room, she is shocked to find it empty. "What the...," but does not get to finish her sentence as Jethro lunges at her from behind the door and wrestles her to the ground, knocking the syringe out of her hand in the process. "Jack, help," she screams just as another detonation rocks the castle. Realizing that she is on her own, she throws Jethro off her and crawls towards the syringe. As she reaches out her hand, Jethro grabs her foot and pulls her back. "No you stinking zombie, get off me!" she screams as Jethro continues to pull himself up her leg. Kicking him in the face, she reaches behind her, franticly searching for the syringe but as she lays her hand on it, Jethro sinks his teeth into her leg. "No...," screaming she plunges the syringe into the back of Jethro's neck and pushes him off her. Quickly grabbing the second syringe she plunges it into her own leg as she feels the zombie virus coursing through her blood vessels.

*****

As Jack patches one hole, another is blown in the other side of the castle. Running across the courtyard another explosion rips the side of the wall at the opposite side. Oh no, I can't fix them both, he thinks running to the furthest hole. Looking out across the field, he gasps at the sight of dozens of creepers moving towards the castle. "Natasha, hurry up. We don't have much time here," he shouts as he patches the hole and runs towards the next as another explosion detonates.

"Natasha, come on girl, we need to get moving!" he shouts at her as she stumbles into the courtyard. "Did you hear me? There are dozens of creepers heading for the castle, did it work, the cure?" he asks just as Jethro also stumbles into the courtyard. They both stare at him with dead eyes, weaving from side to side. "No.... Natasha!" Running towards her she suddenly starts coughing and falls to her knees as Jack arrives at her side.

"Jack, it works. Jethro will be fine but I've bad news. He bit me before I could inject him and I had to use the last syringe on myself. I'm so sorry."

Standing, just as another detonation rips some more of the wall away, Jacks looks at her, tears streaming down his face. "But what about Jay and Nathan. We don't have time to find some more cures and if they stay here the creepers will blow this place apart and they'll burn in the sun."

Struggling to her feet, Natasha reaches out to Jack. "I'm so sorry; I don't know what to say."

"Get off me."

"Jack, it's not her fault. If I hadn't bitten her, we would be ok," stutters Jethro.

"Shut it Jethro." Looking back, Jack looks at him in shock."Jethro, you're ok. Good to have you back." Looking back at Natasha his anger recedes and he apologizes. "Sorry Natasha, but what are we going to do?"

"It's ok Jack, but I just don't know. If only we had some iron ingots we could make some more cure."

"Uh, I have an iron ingot," replies Jethro reaching into his inventory and pulling out the bar.

Running to his side Jack embraces him. "Jethro, you rock man. Quick Natasha, make another syringe."

Throwing the iron ingot to Natasha, she catches it and sets up the crafting table. "Jack, go fill those holes. If the creepers get in here we'll never be able to help them." Working furiously she assembles another syringe then loads it with zombie virus cure.

"Right, Jack keep filling those holes, I'm going to inject Nathan."

"No...What about Jay?"

"We have to do Nathan first. He's carrying the last iron ingot. If we inject Jay then Nathan is dead."

"Right, just do it, just please help Jay too," he pleads.

"I will Jack, I promise. Jethro, come with me. I'm going to need your help with Nathan."

Running into the tower, they stand outside the room as another explosion rocks the castle.

"Right Jethro, when I open the door you have to distract Nathan so I can plunge this syringe into him. Do not let him bite you. We have no more zombie cure, ok?"

"No problem there Natasha. Being infected once was quite enough."

Opening the door Jethro runs into the room and grabs Nathan by the arm, swinging him around to face the far wall. "Now Natasha, get him," he shouts, trying to keep Nathan from biting his upraised arms.

Natasha dashes into the room and plunges the syringe into Nathan's back as he reaches for Jethro.

Letting out an ear-splitting scream, he throws Jethro to the floor and turns to face Natasha. With drool running from his teeth, he advances on her as she stumbles and falls to the floor. Taking advantage of the situation, Nathan lunges at her and jumps on her leg, raising his head ready to deliver a deadly bite.

"Not again," screams Natasha as she raises her free leg, ready to kick Nathan in the head. Just as she is about to release a neck breaking blow Nathan looks at her and smiles.

"Natasha? What are we doing on the floor?"

Laughing despite herself she replies. "Nathan, am I ever glad to see you." Pulling herself to her feet, she picks Nathan up off the floor. "No time for explanations Nate, but do you have an iron ingot in your inventory?"

Reaching inside himself, he pulls out an iron ingot. "Sure, what do you need that for?"

Grabbing the bar, Natasha whips out her crafting table, assembles another syringe, and loads it up with zombie virus cure. "Right Jethro, ready to try that again?"

"Let's do it, uh maybe you can go outside and help Jack mend the walls Nate."

"I'm on it!" he replies running out the door as another explosion rocks the building.

Standing outside Jay's door, they look at each other, and then Jethro swings the door open and charges into the room. Standing against the far wall, Jay looks at them with hungry eyes just as another explosion blows out the back wall and throws everyone to the ground. Pulling herself from the rubble, Natasha sees Jay stumble up as sunlight streaks through the newly made opening. As Natasha screams a warning to Jethro, Jay bursts into flames.

*****

Running into the courtyard Nathan sees Jack franticly building walls. "Jack, what do you want me to do?"

"Nate? Cool, you ok?"

"Yeah I'm fine."

"How about Jay?"

"They're giving him the cure now, he should be fine."

"Great Nate, so glad you're back in the world of the living. Start repairing the walls but stay well back, you never know where another creeper is going to blow."

"I'm on it Jack," shouts Nate, delighted to be back with his friend.

Rushing to a hole, he starts laying blocks.

"Nate, just go two blocks high, nothing can get over that and it saves time."

"You sure Jack? Seems like there's still a big hole," replies Nate.

"Yeah, Natasha taught me."

"Ok cool," he replies moving onto another gaping hole in the wall.

*****

Running straight at Jay, Natasha dives on him and stabs the syringe into his neck. "Jethro, a little help."

Running over, Jethro grabs Jay and helps drag him into the shade, and the flames immediately extinguish.

"Come on Jay, hold in there," extols Natasha holding him down. Slowly he stops shaking, opens his eyes, and says."Argh"

"Oh no Jay..."

"Argh, get off of me will you? You're crushing me!"

"Jay? You're alright?" Throwing herself on him, she gives him a huge hug. "I thought I had lost you."

"Yeah, well I'm fine, nice to see you too Natasha."

Suddenly embarrassed, she jumps off him and helps him up. "Well, good to have you back. Come on we need to help Jack."

Slapping him on his back, Jethro congratulates Jay. "Good to see you Jay, I thought you were a goner for sure."

"Nah, you can't get me that easily, although being a zombie was no picnic."

"I know just what you mean."

"What, you too?"

"Afraid so, Nate too. It seems Jack and Natasha saved us all."

"No way, for real? Little Jack saved everyone?"

"It would appear so, yes."

"Way to go Jack, where is he anyway?"

As another detonation splits the air, Jethro replies. "He's outside, repairing the walls. It seems we're under attack from creepers."

"Oh no," shouts Jay rushing out of the tower. As he leaves, a creeper rushes in through the hole in the wall, heading straight for Jethro and starting to glow, a sure sign that he is about to explode. Diving through the door and slamming it behind him, Jethro dashes out of the tower as the wall behind him explodes, sending him flying through the air. Scrambling to his feet, he runs back to the entrance and places blocks across the opening. Looking about, he sees Jay and Natasha standing on the wall looking out across the field. Joining them on the battlements, he interrupts their conversation.

"Uh people, you might not have noticed but we're under attack here."

Just pointing out over the battlements Jay replies. "Look!"

Looking out, Jethro gives a gasp. "But how is this possible? I've never seen this many Creepers before."

"Who knows, it must be another mod pack. Maybe we missed it with all the explosions taking place, but we can't defend against that. We need to evacuate, now."

Jumping from the wall, he runs in the direction of Jack and Nate shouting. "Guys, we're leaving, grab anything useful, and meet by the back wall in one minute."

"What's up Jay, we can defend, just keep repairing the walls."

"No time now to discuss it, just be there in one minute, now move."

Running back to the tower, he grabs the furnace and crafting table that

Natasha left outside and prepares to leave. Jumping from the wall, Natasha and Jethro look from one to another.

"So Jay, what's the plan?"

"Head for the coast, creepers can't swim. Maybe we can find an island or something."

"Yeah, but you saw what was out there, how we going to get there?"

"Over the back wall, the field is relatively clear, just a few creepers. As long as we move fast, we should be able to stay ahead of them. Right, let's move," he shouts as Nathan and Jack run up. "Over the back wall and head for the coast where we'll make a boat and get away from this nightmare."

Jumping to their feet, they climb the wall and drop on the other side.

"Ready?" asks Jay, looking at each in turn.

"Let's do this," says Jack, holding his hand into the circle.

"Yeah," says Nate, holding his on top of Jack's hand.

Following Jack's lead, the other three place their hands in the centre of the circle and shake.

Breaking, they run across the field, dodging creepers and heading for what they hope is their salvation.

*****

Here ends the first book in the Masters of Minecraft Series.

Book 1 - Masters Of Minecraft - The Awakening

Book 2 - Masters Of Minecraft- The Invasion

CPSIA information can be obtained at www.ICGtesting.com
Printed in the USA
LVOW04s0848170814

399533LV00002B/223/P